RETHINKING
"ONE CHINA"

Mike Chen
12/14/04

重估"一個中國"政策

RETHINKING "ONE CHINA"

Edited by John J. Tkacik, Jr.

© 2004 by The Heritage Foundation
214 Massachusetts Avenue, NE
Washington, DC 20002-4999
(202) 546-4400 • heritage.org

Printed in the United States of America

ISBN: 0-89195-270-5

Contents

1

Introduction: Rethinking "One China"

JOHN J. TKACIK, JR.

THIS BOOK IS THE RESULT OF A FEBRUARY 26, 2004, HERITAGE Foundation symposium, "Rethinking 'One China,'" which addressed the "one China" dilemma in American foreign policy. Symposium panelists included two of America's most respected China scholars (Arthur Waldron of the University of Pennsylvania and Ross Terrill of Harvard); two thoughtful strategic thinkers (Thomas Donnelly of the American Enterprise Institute and William Kristol of the Project for the New American Century); and myself. A last-minute emergency prevented Bill Kristol from speaking on his panel, but his thoughts are encapsulated in a paper that he presented at a congressional hearing on April 21, 2004, and which is included in this volume.

Also participating in the symposium project and discussions were five members of the U.S. House of Representatives: the two co-chairmen of the Congressional Taiwan Caucus, Representatives Steve Chabot (R–OH) and Dana Rohrabacher (R–CA), and Representatives Peter Deutsch (D–FL), Joseph M. Hoeffel (D–PA), and Robert E. Andrews (D–NJ). Additional remarks on the "One China" issue by Representatives Andrews and Chabot, delivered in September 2003 and published as a Heritage Foundation *Lecture*, add extra dimensions to the debate and are included in this volume as well.

The unifying theme of these chapters is the risk inherent in basing a foreign policy on myth, because "One China" is one of the true-blue myths of late 20th century diplomacy. The contributors look at the reality: Two separate countries now face each other across the Taiwan Strait. One is the emerging Chinese superpower on the Asian mainland, and the other is the young Taiwanese democracy in the island rim of the Western Pacific. Whereas these two lands are increasingly entwined in the trade, banking, and economic networks that interconnect all of East Asia, their politics and society are increasingly disparate.

"One China" has been a shibboleth of American diplomacy for a half-century (or longer, if one considers that "territorial integrity of China" that was a mainstay of U.S. China policy in the pre–World War II decades). But it is a shibboleth that has been construed differently in Beijing, Taipei, and Washington. In Beijing, it has always meant that China is sovereign over Taiwan and has the firm right in international law to seize the island by force whenever it is able to amass the capacity to do so. In Taipei, it once justified Chiang Kai-shek's orders to keep the island on a war footing for an ultimate military counterattack against the rebel Communists on the mainland. But it no longer means that. In fact, the words "one China" have been banished from Taipei's diplomatic lexicon since July 1999.

In Washington, the words never meant anything other than that the United States recognizes one government of China at a time. Legally, the United States treats Taiwan as it treats all other "foreign countries, nations, states, governments, or similar entities"[1] for the purposes of domestic law. Militarily, Taiwan has been America's largest market for defense equipment. Diplomatically, however, Taiwan's constitution still mandates that the country's official name is the "Republic of China," and so long as that is the case, the United States cannot recognize it.

Taipei cannot simply resolve the matter by declaring to Beijing, "That's it: You won the civil war, you're China, and we're not," and

---

[1] The Taiwan Relations Act (Public Law 96–8; see Appendix B in this volume), signed by President Carter on April 10, 1979.

then go its peaceful way. This may have been possible in 1971 when Taiwan's vice foreign minister Yang Hsi-kun explained that Taiwan's expulsion from the United Nations was an effort by Beijing "to force international recognition of [China's] right to take over Taiwan as an integral part of China." Yang secretly asked the U.S. ambassador for American pressure on Chiang Kai-shek to declare Taiwan's independence under the name of "the Chinese Republic of Taiwan." Japan's prime minister, added Yang, had already made such an approach to Chiang Kai-shek, but to no avail.[2] But the international situation in the intervening decades now restrains Taiwan from moving unilaterally or without broad international approbation.

Nor can Beijing legitimize its use of force against Taiwan by insisting it is a "breakaway" province in open rebellion against the lawful national government.

Nor can Washington solve the matter with a continuous and unthinking repetition of the "one China" mantra, because this risks willful misreading in Beijing. After President George W. Bush's repeated assurances to Chinese leaders that he "opposed" Taiwanese independence (as if Taiwan were not already independent), Bonnie Glaser, a respected American China scholar, reported that:

> Some Chinese even believe that there is sufficient concern in Washington about Chen's actions and his future agenda that the U.S. may acquiesce in a limited use of force by the PLA—for example, to seize an offshore island, temporarily impose a limited blockade, or fire a lone missile at a military target on Taiwan.[3]

---

[2] See Department of State Telegram 71 Taipei 5869, from the Ambassador in Taipei to the Secretary of State, "Subject: Conversation of Vice Minister Yang Hsi-kun with Ambassador," November 30, 1971, classified "Secret–Nodis–eyes only for the Secretary and Assistant Secretary Green."

[3] Bonnie S. Glaser, "Washington's Hands-On Approach to Managing Cross-Strait Tension," PacNet Number 21, Pacific Forum CSIS Honolulu, Hawaii, May 13, 2004, at *www.csis.org/pacfor/pac0421.pdf*.

With the re-election of Taiwan's pro-independence president, Chen Shui-bian, in March 2004, there are two new strategic realities in the Strait. Independence is now a mainstream political sentiment on the island, and China is rapidly building an advanced military force strong enough to destroy Taiwan as a political entity unless Taiwan is assisted by the United States.

America's main challenge in the coming century will be to manage a rising China. The views and opinions expressed in these pages, by scholars and political leaders alike, make a persuasive case that the challenge is made more complex—not easier—by continuing a "one China" policy.

2

Confronting Reality: There Are Two Chinas

THE HONORABLE STEVE CHABOT

IN HIS SEMINAL SPEECH AT WHITEHALL PALACE IN LONDON ON November 19, 2003, President George W. Bush outlined "Three Pillars" of global peace and security.[1] The first pillar, he said, is that "international organizations must be equal to the challenges facing our world, from lifting up failing states to opposing proliferation." The second is the "willingness of free nations, when the last resort arrives, to restrain aggression and evil by force." And the third pillar of security is "our commitment to the global expansion of democracy, and the hope and progress it brings."

The "One China Principle," for which Beijing's leaders say they are willing to wage war, challenges all three of these pillars. Beijing's "Principle" posits that "there is only one China in the world, Taiwan is an inalienable part of China, and the seat of China's central government is in Beijing."[2] Taiwan's government, the Chinese say, "has always remained only a local authority in Chinese territory."[3]

As such, the "One China Principle" is an affront to all three of these "Pillars" of global security.

This chapter is an adaptation of remarks prepared by Representative Chabot for a symposium, "Rethinking 'One China': A Fiction More Dangerous Than Useful?" held at The Heritage Foundation on February 26, 2004.

First, Beijing blocks Taiwan's participation in virtually all international organizations, and in the few forums that do include Taiwan, such as the World Trade Organization, the Asian Development Bank, and the Asia–Pacific Economic Cooperation forum,
China violates the terms of its own participation whenever it pres-
sures those organizations to limit Taiwan's status. Although Taiwan has advanced nuclear, chemical, and biotech industries, and
manufactures conventional arms and missiles, China has blocked
Taiwan from participating in any international nonproliferation
regime. The United States has acquiesced, despite China's repu-
tation as the world's biggest proliferator of weapons of mass
destruction and their delivery systems.[4]

Second, the authoritarian regime in Beijing continues to threat-
en war with democratic Taiwan unless Taiwan joins China under
the same "one country, two systems" formula that governs Hong
Kong and Macau. At some point, China's aggressiveness may have
to be restrained by force.

Third, the United States stands for the global expansion of
democracy. Taiwan is one of Asia's most dynamic and vibrant
democracies, and the United States must support that democracy.

---

[1] Office of the White House Press Secretary, "Remarks by the President at Whitehall
Palace Royal Banqueting House—Whitehall Palace, London, England," November 19,
2003, at *www.whitehouse.gov/news/releases/2003/11/20031119-1.html.*

[2] State Council of the People's Republic of China, Taiwan Affairs Office and Information Office, *The Taiwan Question and the Reunification of China,* August 31, 1993. English text from Xinhua News Agency.

[3] State Council of the People's Republic of China, Taiwan Affairs Office, *The Principle
of One China and the Taiwan Question,* February 21, 2000. English text from Xinhua News
Agency and *People's Daily.*

[4] China provided nuclear weapons designs to Pakistan, which then transferred them
to Libya. See Joby Warrick and Peter Slevin, "Libyan Arms Designs Traced Back to China,
Pakistanis Resold Chinese-Provided Plans," *The Washington Post,* February 15, 2004, p.
A1, at *www.washingtonpost.com/wp-dyn/articles/A42692-2004Feb14.html.* The Rumsfeld
Commission reported in July 1998 that China "poses a threat as a significant proliferator
of ballistic missiles, weapons of mass destruction, and enabling technologies." See U.S.
House of Representatives, *Report of the Commission to Assess the Ballistic Missile Threat to the
United States,* July 15, 1998, at *www.fas.org/irp/threat/bm-threat.htm.* The Cox Committee
asserted in its May 1999 report that "[t]he PRC has proliferated nuclear, missile, and
space-related technologies to a number of countries. The PRC is one of the leading pro-
liferators of complete ballistic missile systems and missile components in the world." See

By accepting Beijing's "One China Principle," the United States would in fact legitimize China's threat to use force against Taiwan. For the past decade, lip service to "One China" has become an increasingly risky stance because it encourages Beijing to believe that the United States will not defend a Taiwan that seeks an identity separate from China's.

Henry Kissinger's opening to China 30 years ago had its rationale. For 17 years, from about 1972 to February 15, 1989, when the last Soviet tank crossed "Friendship Bridge" over the Amu Darya River and out of Afghanistan, the United States and China had maintained an effective strategic partnership. Indeed, through the 1980s, China was liberalizing and the Communist Party was reforming.

But when Chinese troops massacred defenseless Buddhist monks who demonstrated in Lhasa on March 12, 1989, and when over 400,000 Chinese People's Liberation Army troops were called into Beijing to face down a million and a half Chinese civilians demonstrating for democracy and against corruption in Tiananmen Square in June 1989, the Chinese Communist Party's political reforms ceased.

At once, the United States and China ceased to share a vision of political liberalization. And when the Soviet Union disintegrated on New Year's Eve 1991, the United States and China no longer shared a strategic vision. The different ways that Washington and Beijing reacted strategically to the Soviet collapse proved this.

With the Soviet threat gone, the United States immediately set about reaping a "peace dividend," with defense expenditures dropping over 10 percent, from $298 billion in fiscal year 1992

U.S. House of Representatives, *U.S. National Security and Military/Commercial Concerns with the People's Republic of China*, May 25, 1999, p. xxxvi, at *www.house.gov/coxreport/*. In January 2000, the CIA identified China as a "key supplier" of WMD and delivery technologies: "During the reporting period, firms in China provided missile-related items, raw materials, and/or assistance to several countries of proliferation concern—such as Iran. China also was a supplier of ACW [advanced conventional weapons] to Iran...." See U.S. Central Intelligence Agency, *Unclassified Report to Congress on the Acquisition of Technology Relating to Weapons of Mass Destruction and Advanced Conventional Munitions: 1 January through 30 June 1999*, at *www.cia.gov/cia/reports/archive/reports_1999.html.*

to $268 billion in fiscal year 1997.[5] On the other hand, China's Communist Party turned its sights on the newly democratic Taiwan. Taiwan's new democracy, it seems, is more of a threat to China's despots than the Soviet Union was. In the same period, Chinese defense spending sustained annual double-digit increases. The Pentagon estimates total defense-related expenditures in 2004 to be between $50 billion and $70 billion, ranking China third in defense spending after the United States and Russia.[6]

My concern is that as long as China claims Taiwan as its territory, the Chinese Communist Party cannot tolerate Taiwan's democracy unless it is subservient (like Hong Kong's dimming liberalism) to the dictates of the Party center in Beijing. Yet I worry that American policy has been to humor China, to soothe China's temper, to cajole China to behave itself with constant reassurances that we have a "one China" policy.

In secret, American diplomats will admit that America's "one China" policy really doesn't mean that Taiwan is part of China. They say, "the matter of Taiwan's sovereignty should be resolved by people on both sides of the Taiwan Strait."

But China never hears that. China has been led to think that America's "one China" policy means that the United States recognizes that Taiwan is "part of China," just as Chechnya is part of Russia, or Biafra was part of Nigeria, or Aceh is part of Indonesia. In Beijing, America's "one China" policy legitimizes Beijing's threats to use force and even encourages them.

In other words, to be blunt, our so-called one China policy is dangerous.

---

[5] U.S. Office of Management and Budget, *The Budget for Fiscal Year 2005: Historical Tables*, pp. 49–51, select from menu at *www.gpoaccess.gov/usbudget/fy05/browse.html.* [Ed. note: the U.S. Department of State lists China's annual military expenditures as second only to those of the United States. See "World Military Expenditures and Arms Transfers 1999–2000," released June 2002, p. 38, at *www.state.gov/t/vc/rls/rpt/wmeat/1999_2000/*, and *www.state.gov/documents/organization/18738.pdf.*]

[6] Richard P. Lawless, testimony before the Subcommittee on East Asian and Pacific Affairs, Committee on Foreign Relations, U.S. Senate, April 26, 2004, at *http://foreign.senate.gov/testimony/2004/LawlessTestimony040422.pdf.*

Taiwan is already an independent, sovereign nation. No amount of diplomatic double-talk can obscure this fact. It is time to recognize this reality fully. Taiwan has a population of 23 million people, making it bigger than 80 percent of the countries represented in the United Nations.

Taiwan is a democracy, but that is a fact that is vulnerable to belittling by American diplomats and politicians who fear some kind of backlash from China.

Taiwan is a valued trading partner, ranking as America's eighth-largest export market in 2003; but American policies that encourage Taiwan's high-tech industries, especially their semiconductor factories, to move to China (as I saw recently on the front page of *The Wall Street Journal*[7]), as though this somehow lessens China's hostility against Taiwan, are misguided. Soon the same computer chips that power the most advanced American weapons will be produced (and designed) in Chinese facilities—facilities, I should point out, that are at the disposal of China's Army.

I am all for dialogue. Taiwan's President Chen Shui-bian has shown great flexibility in his approach to the Taiwan Strait issue, calling for a peaceful dialogue of equals with his Chinese counterparts. But American policymakers seem to think that Taiwan is the problem. In fact, it is the Chinese side that is unbending in its demand that Taiwan submit as a part of China before any dialogue can take place. Beijing has been unyielding because their leaders are convinced that Washington's "one China" policy supports them.

We need to think outside the box, as they say, about Taiwan. That means we must either spell out our "one China" policy so that the world knows that it means only that the United States recognizes one government of China at a time, or dump the "one China" slogan altogether. At this point, I urge the latter.

As a Member of Congress, the national interests of the United States are uppermost in my mind. I believe it is in America's

---

[7] Jason Dean, "Beijing Dangles Fat Incentives to Lure Plants, Know-How; Taiwanese at the Helm; Mr. Chang's Dream Foundry," *The Wall Street Journal*, February 17, 2004, at *http://online.wsj.com/article/0,,SB107696027203830630,00.html.*

interests to recognize Taiwan for the independent country that it is. Peace and stability in East Asia are best served by the United States having a good relationship with both China and Taiwan. China's delusion that the world thinks Taiwan is an alienated part of China only emboldens Beijing's tyrants to think that the Western democracies, led by the United States, will do nothing.

History is replete with instances of large and powerful tyrannies intimidating their neighbors, and history is replete with instances where the principled nations of the world stood by and did nothing until it was too late. And history is replete with instances where emboldened tyrannies, their appetites unsatisfied by smaller conquests, moved on until major wars were ignited.

Britain and France abandoned democratic Austria and then democratic Czechoslovakia in 1938; the West did not lift a finger to shield Israel from its Arab neighbors in 1948. In 1979, the Soviet Union occupied Afghanistan because it guessed that the West would do little; in the end, Afghanistan was in ruins, and the primeval chaos of Afghanistan became the breeding ground of global terrorism. Saddam Hussein simply assumed that the United States would not aid Kuwait in 1990 because the U.S. policy was to "take no position on Arab–Arab territorial disputes."

It is time for the United States to take an explicit stand on the China–China territorial dispute. It is time to make it clear that we see not "one China" but two nations that have emerged from the Chinese civil war of 1949. I am proud to say that I have been pushing for a reassessment of the "one China" policy for years, and I am happy to share the stage with liberals and conservatives, Democrats and Republicans, who believe in democracy, in resisting aggression, and in a Taiwanese people that is free to determine its own destiny.

3

The Taiwan Relations Act:
The Next 25 Years

AS MEMBERS OF CONGRESS CONSIDER ISSUES RELATING TO China and Taiwan, they might begin by considering something a "senior Administration official" said last week about our policy on Israeli settlements and Palestinian refugees. "Eliminating taboos and saying the truth about the situation is, we think, a contribution toward peace. Getting people to face reality in this situation is going to help, not hurt."[1]

This statement applies equally to the Taiwan Strait. America's policy toward Taiwan is ridden with taboos. In fact, one such taboo is the virtual prohibition on questioning whether our interests and those of democratic Taiwan are served by the various communiqués agreed to by Beijing and Washington since 1972. This reluctance to adjust U.S. policy to reflect changes in the strategic and political situation in the region has also meant that the Taiwan Relations Act itself has never substantively been amended.[2]

Today, and in the coming months, we need an honest and public discussion of what we want to happen and not to happen

---

This presentation was made before the Committee on International Relations, U.S. House of Representatives, on April 21, 2004, and is available at *http://wwwc.house.gov/ international_relations/108/Krio42104.htm*. It is included in this volume with the permission of the author.

in China and in Taiwan. We have for many years avoided such a discussion. It has been as if Taiwan's survival as a democracy, and, for that matter China's possible evolution into one, are not proper matters of polite conversation. Instead, we have pretended that there can be an unchanging "status quo," that China is not seriously preparing for military action or other forms of coercion against Taiwan, and that Taiwan's people would be amenable to unification if it were handled well.

Congress passed the Taiwan Relations Act to avert the worst consequences of President Jimmy Carter's decision in 1978 to break relations with Taipei, withdraw U.S. troops, and abrogate the mutual defense treaty. The TRA established important principles of U.S. policy—chiefly our insistence on a peaceful resolution of Taiwan's fate, our opposition to aggression, including coercive acts such as boycotts or embargoes, and a commitment to Taiwan's defense through the provision of defensive arms and the maintenance of America's own ability to resist Chinese aggression against Taiwan. As you know, Congress also established a role for itself in providing for Taiwan's defense needs and in determining any response to a danger that the President is required to report under the Act.

The "one China" policy and the strategic ambiguity that came to govern U.S. policy are nowhere to be found in the law's text. Yet, as any observer of U.S. China policy knows, the language of "one China" pervades U.S. policy. It is a mantra that every official must intone on virtually any occasion on which China or Taiwan is discussed.

The "one China" policy began as a way to defer the resolution of Taiwan's fate until better conditions for resolving it prevailed. It purposely left the U.S. neutral about the outcome.

Unfortunately, the policy has come to mean denying Taiwanese sovereignty and self-determination. Part of the problem is that the arcane and nuanced language that its advocates believe

---

[1] Peter Slevin, "Delicate Maneuvers Led to U.S.–Israeli Stance," *The Washington Post*, April 16, 2004, p. A1.

[2] The Taiwan Relations Act is Public Law 96–8 (United States Code, Title 22, Chapter 48, Sections 3301–3316), enacted April 10, 1979. Text is at Appendix B in this volume.

manages a complicated situation—and deters the non-expert from trying to criticize it—does not reflect the changes that have taken place on both sides of the Strait. It also invites constant pressure for revisions from Beijing. For example, over the past year, Beijing has campaigned to bring about a change in U.S. policy from "not supporting" Taiwan independence to "opposing it." Officially, "not supporting" independence remains U.S. policy.

This apparently slight difference is actually important. Not supporting Taiwan's independence is consistent with longstanding policy of not predetermining the outcome of discussions or negotiations between China and Taiwan. Opposing independence appears to settle the matter and might give Beijing reason to believe that the U.S. might not resist China's use of force against Taiwan or coercive measures designed to bring about a capitulation of sovereignty.

At the same time, independence sentiment on the part of Taiwan's people is neither frivolous nor provocative, but rather the natural manifestation of a process that the U.S. has supported. As my colleague Gary Schmitt wrote recently in *The Wall Street Journal*:

> Taiwanese identity has grown in direct relation to the progress of democracy on the island. The people of Taiwan increasingly have come to think of themselves as Taiwanese as they have established themselves over the past decade as a self-governing people."[3]

Viewed this way, Taiwan's desirable democratic transformation has an unavoidable implication for U.S. policy on Taiwan—not to tilt against independence but toward it.

In short, the "one China" policy expresses neither the situation on the ground in Taiwan nor U.S. values and interests. No one drafting a new U.S. policy toward Taiwan today would recreate the

---

[3] Gary Schmitt, "Taiwan's Democracy Needs Support, Not Benign Neglect," *The Wall Street Journal*, March 23, 2004, p. A22.

one the U.S. has pursued since the 1970s and 1980s. Ever since its basic premises were set forth, the policy has been under pressure. The reason is obvious: The situation has changed. Taiwan's people have established democracy. More important, they no longer claim the mainland or wish to join it. Even the Kuomintang—the Nationalist Party—has abandoned its longstanding position regarding unification.

Meanwhile, across the Strait, economic growth has fueled China's military modernization. There are at least 450 missiles pointed at Taiwan, and Beijing is acquiring other capabilities designed to help it take Taiwan or coerce Taiwan to accept unification on Beijing's terms. China's leaders rely increasingly on nationalism, rather than communism, as the source of legitimacy for the regime. This will become more pronounced if, as predicted, labor unrest, the banking system, and the further collapse of state enterprises become more dire problems.

Future policy on Taiwan should be designed to reflect new realities. In the short term, we can take practical steps that reflect Taiwan's importance as a fellow democracy, maximize its international standing, and improve U.S.–Taiwan defense cooperation.

Bilateral Relations

The U.S. should reduce Taiwan's international isolation by increasing high-level contacts. The number of visits to Taipei and to Washington by senior officials should be increased to the point that it is unremarkable.

The Administration must soon decide who will represent the United States at the upcoming inauguration of President Chen for his second term. It would be good to send someone of prestige and importance, especially in light of the Administration's handling of the congratulations to President Chen on his re-election. This is a perfect opportunity for the Administration to signal Beijing that the future of U.S.–Taiwan relations will be more respectful of Taiwan's democratic character.

It would help if Washington sent an Administration official of high rank from within the Bush Administration. Serving Cabinet members have visited Taiwan in the past, but none have visited Taiwan since 1998 when Secretary of Energy Bill Richardson was trapped in a high-rise hotel during an earthquake. Why shouldn't the Bush Administration send a Cabinet officer to represent the U.S. at the May inauguration ceremony?

Washington should also change the way it deals with the president of Taiwan. While the visits of Taiwan's presidents have been increasingly dignified, the *ad hoc* nature of the policy on visits guarantees intense pressure from China and forces the U.S. to devote unreasonable amounts of effort to placating Beijing.

It is frankly absurd that a democratically elected president cannot visit senior U.S. officials or even Washington, but general secretaries of the Chinese Communist Party have been to the White House. Taiwanese officials below the level of the president also need to be able to come to the U.S. and speak freely to the American public and the media. The fact that they do not may not be due to any particular policy directive. However, it is undeniably true that Taiwan's international isolation has created ingrained habits—both here and in Taipei—that are extremely unhealthy and even counterproductive insofar as they prevent a frank sharing of views.

Defense and Regional Security

After the 1995 and 1996 missile volleys, the U.S. realized we were ill-prepared to coordinate defense of Taiwan with Taiwan's own defense forces. Since that time, we have improved our preparations. These efforts should be continued, enhanced, and made as public as possible to underscore our commitment to Taiwan's defense. Greater openness about the nature and extent of America's commitment to Taiwan's defense would help deter Beijing and dispel ambiguity. Such openness would also benefit the people of the United States who, far from fearing America's overseas commitments, understand the importance of America's defending democratic allies.

Furthermore, Taiwan is more than just a dependent. It also cooperates with America's security objectives. Last August, on receiving a request by the U.S., Taiwan forced a North Korean freighter to unload dual-use chemicals. According to an American official, "we provided the intelligence and Taiwan stepped up to the plate."

In short, Taiwan is helping the Proliferation Security Initiative, an effort the Bush Administration launched to stop nuclear proliferation. Taiwan should be allowed to join the core group of the PSI, which just recently added three new members. Incidentally, according to the State Department, the PSI is "an activity, not an organization," so the question of statehood for membership is not an issue. By virtue of its democratic character, its strategic location, and its long history of working with the United States, Taiwan's cooperation in regional security is imperative to U.S. interests. There is no reason that Taiwan should not be recognized as a participant not only in PSI, but also in other multilateral discussions, exercises, and operations among democratic countries in Asia.

U.S. efforts to draw Taiwan into the international community should also include a serious initiative to win Taiwan's admission into the World Health Organization, including sponsoring its nomination for membership. Taiwan's exclusion from the WHO vastly complicated efforts to deal with the spread of SARS. No one has forgotten the callous comment of the Chinese ambassador after Taiwan failed to win admission to the WHO as an observer last year: "The bid is rejected. Who cares about your Taiwan?"

The Bush Administration has expressed its support for Taiwan's WHO membership. China, however, is uniquely talented at using leverage and threats in international fora, and the WHO is no exception. The U.S. and other sympathetic countries need to meet China's ante and raise it.

Finally, a free trade agreement between the U.S. and Taiwan would fit neatly within U.S. policy to build bilateral trade agreements. The Project for the New American Century held a conference on this idea and found wide acceptance of the idea within the policy and business communities of both our countries. Politically, the impact would be extremely important.

With regard to China, we need to be quite clear that we expect Beijing not to attack or coerce Taiwan in any way, and that the costs to Beijing of attacking Taiwan would be more than it can bear. We also need to be clear that we look forward to China becoming a democratic country like Taiwan. Then the people on each side of the Strait can decide their relationship and their future.

When Vice President Richard Cheney visited China on April 15, he made an impressive speech that spoke about democracy. But the Vice President used one key word that let China know that, for now, the U.S. does not consider democracy a priority for China. That word is "eventually." Cheney said China's people will "eventually ask why they cannot be trusted with decisions over what to say and what to believe."

"Eventually" was used with precision not only in this speech, but also in President Bush's widely praised speech establishing democracy as a foreign policy priority to the National Endowment for Democracy last November. America's policy toward China is insufficiently directed toward democratizing China, and so long as that is true, it will be more difficult to help Taiwan's democracy survive.

Conclusion

Twenty five years ago, Congress checked the Carter Administration's policy on Taiwan. At the time, to quote one scholar, Beijing hoped that the U.S. withdrawal of support "would arouse a sufficient sense of vulnerability within the Nationalist government to make it more susceptible to overtures from the mainland." Beijing decided that, "If Taiwan would only bow to Beijing's sovereignty, then the Beijing government would promise to concede a very high degree of administrative autonomy to the Taipei authorities. The 'two systems,' Communism on the mainland and capitalism on Taiwan, could then co-exist within a single country"[4] The famous "one

---

[4] Robert Cottrell, *The End of Hong Kong: The Secret Diplomacy of Imperial Retreat* (London: John Murray, 1993), p. 60.

country, two systems" formula that China claims to apply in Hong Kong was originally dreamed up with Taiwan in mind.

It didn't work. Congress acted to pass the Taiwan Relations Act, and China set its sights on Hong Kong. Since 1997, it has been quite clear that Beijing is not interested in or sincere about respecting autonomy under a "one country, two systems" arrangement.

Don't misunderstand. America's commitment to Taiwan is admirable. No other country could or would do what the United States has done. At the same time, no other country except the U.S. can hurt Taiwan or weaken it as much as the United States can.

The greatest test is still to come. China is very serious about taking Taiwan, and we have not done enough to dissuade it. Taiwan has transformed itself from a dictatorship to a democracy. That momentous change has very likely increased the chances of a conflict in the Taiwan Strait—not because Taiwan is provocative, but because China cannot abide Taiwan's democratic character and the reality that it has become a separate, self-governing people. That is why U.S. clarity and resolve are so important.

A discussion of these and other issues needs to happen now and yield results right away. The Pentagon has estimated that the balance of forces in the Taiwan Strait will begin to tip in Beijing's favor, perhaps as soon as next year. We need above all, therefore, to deter any attack or coercion. And we need to rethink policy constraints developed for circumstances decades ago while confronting greatly changed and still changing conditions in order to develop a new, sustainable policy for security and democracy in Taiwan and China for the present and future.

4

American Diplomacy, and the Origins of Cross-Strait Tensions

ARTHUR WALDRON

To begin, it is important to understand that Washington means something quite different from what Beijing means when it speaks of "one China." For Beijing, the phrase means, in the words of the Constitution of 1993, that "Taiwan is part of the sacred territory of the People's Republic of China." This is a view that the United States has never accepted.

Thus, President Bill Clinton's press secretary, Mike McCurry, had to retract when he responded erroneously in a September 1994 press conference to the question whether the U.S. Administration considered Taiwan a part of China: "Absolutely. It's—that's been a consistent feature of our one-China."[1] In the following year, he modified this to the correct position: namely, that "We [the United States] certainly acknowledge *the Chinese position* [i.e., not the U.S. position] that there is one China and Taiwan is part of China."[2]

Ordinary people are understandably confused when even presidential spokesmen find these diplomatic nuances difficult to follow. But the nuances are crucial, for throughout the negotiations of the

This contribution is an adaptation of remarks prepared for a symposium, "Rethinking 'One China': A Fiction More Dangerous Than Useful?" held at The Heritage Foundation on February 26, 2004.

1970s—even including 1979, when we broke all formal diplomatic
ties with the government of the Republic of China (ROC) on Taiwan—State Department international lawyers had been careful to
conserve the American position, which is that the position of Taiwan under international law has yet to be determined.

When the United States speaks of "one China" (the term was
evidently introduced into the diplomatic lexicon by an ill-judged
letter sent by Winston Lord during the Clinton Administration[3]),
we mean no more than that at any time we recognize only one
government as the government of all of China. This position, on
which Beijing insists, is similar to the Hallstein doctrine, which
Bonn once attempted to enforce against East Germany: that states
recognizing East Berlin as a German capital could not have relations with West Germany (a position later abandoned).

Even so—despite Washington's legal agnosticism with respect
to Taiwan's international status—during the period of the 1970s,
when today's China and Taiwan policies were laid out, the expec-
tation was nearly universal that when Washington broke relations
with Taipei, the then-autocratic regime in Taipei would find itself
unable to continue and its leaders, most of whom were Chinese-
born, would grasp the situation and reach over the heads of the
then-disenfrachised Taiwanese people to reach an agreement
returning Taiwan to Beijing under the system of "one country,
two systems" proposed by Deng Xiaoping and return to China to

---

[1] Mike McCurry, "State Department Regular Briefing," Federal News Service, September 8, 1994.

[2] Mike McCurry, Press Briefing, July 13, 1995. Emphasis added.

[3] Julian Baum, "On the Sidelines: Taipei Anxious About US–China Warming," *Far Eastern Economic Review*, November 25, 1993, p. 20. [Ed. note: Although it is true that the term
"one-China policy" was rarely uttered prior to the Clinton Administration, President
George H. W. Bush did use the phrase "one-China policy." See "Remarks to General Dynamics Employees in Fort Worth, Texas," September 2, 1992, in *Public Papers of the Presidents:
Administration of George Bush 1992* (Washington, D.C.: U.S. Government Printing Office,
1994), p. 1470, at *www.presidency.ucsb.edu/pppus.php?admin=041&year=1992&id=090202*.
"We keep our word: our one-China policy, our recognition of the PRC as the sole legitimate government of China. I've always stressed that the importance of the 1982 commu-
niqu[é] on arms sales to Taiwan lies in its promotion of common political goals: peace and
stability in the area through mutual restraint."]

take high, honorific titles in the government. The whole issue would then be rendered moot.

The period when all of this took place was, of course, the 1970s—one of the 20th century's nadirs of American self-confidence and of its confidence in democracy. We were being defeated in Vietnam. Many felt that we had picked the wrong side in that fight—the Republic of Vietnam was no more than an American client state, incapable of independent existence, whereas Hanoi represented the real future of that country.

Much the same view was taken of Taiwan, so much so that no consideration whatsoever was given in government to the possibility that Taiwan might in fact continue to exist indefinitely. What might be called "Plan A" called for it to disappear; the institutions created in 1979 were, in their early drafts, designed to be temporary and deal with a transition (Congress substantially altered the original Carter Administration draft of the Taiwan Relations Act, making it far stronger than the Administration had intended). No "Plan B" was even considered.

In the language of strategic analysis, this sort of approach is called "scripting." That is to say, instead of carefully examining all possible eventualities, the decision maker picks one and then writes a script for it: First we do this, then they do this, and so on until the desired conclusion is reached. The problem turned out to be that Taiwan did not follow the script.

To understand this, imagine that Henry Kissinger had fallen asleep at some point in the mid-1970s and had awakened, say, today at this meeting. Most likely, he would initially find incredible the situation we are discussing: one in which a strong and prosperous Taiwan is governed by a president from the Democratic Progressive Party (an opposition group that did not come into being until November 1986) who is poised to seek a second term in general presidential and parliamentary elections. Kissinger would probably rub his eyes and then ask, incredulously, "Surely, you jest. Surely, Taiwan came to terms with China sometime in the early 1980s, no later." Such were the expectations at the time of "normalization," in both Beijing and Washington.

The degree to which Kissinger shared these expectations is conveyed in one of the more striking passages in his memoirs, in which he sheds the obligatory crocodile tears as he considers what he imagines to be the future. He recalls how, on the very day in 1971 that he was due to leave for his secret mission to Beijing, he encountered none other than Taipei's ambassador, James Shen, who wanted to talk about (as it seemed to Kissinger) some irrelevant issues about whether the ROC could retain a seat in the General Assembly of the United Nations when China joined the Security Council—a vote that was lost 55–53–15 and could probably have been won had Washington understood its importance.

Now the crocodile tears: "No government less deserved what was about to happen to it than that of Taiwan," Kissinger observes. "I found my role with Shen particularly painful, since I knew that before long his esoteric discussion of UN procedural maneuvers would be overtaken by more *elemental events*."[4]

"Elemental events": what a resonant phrase, one that captures the sense shared by all participants that the Nixon diplomacy with China was not simply a matter of achieving tactical balance against the USSR. Rather, it was an exercise in diplomacy on the grandest scale, remaking the world order rather as Kissinger's hero Metternich had done at the Congress of Vienna in 1814–1815.

Kissinger was quite prepared to accept Chinese terms with respect to Taiwan. On meeting Zhou Enlai shortly after arriving in Beijing in 1971, Richard Nixon's envoy launched into a disquisition on geopolitics, only to be repeatedly nudged by John Holdridge, the Foreign Service officer accompanying him, to state the phrase that Beijing required: "that the United States did not seek to create 'two Chinas, one China, one Taiwan, or an independent Taiwan.'" Only upon Kissinger's use of the phrase did Zhou Enlai express approval and indicate that the discussion could begin. (Interestingly, this fact is omitted from Kissinger's memoirs.)[5]

---

[4] Henry Kissinger, *White House Years* (Boston: Little, Brown, 1979), p. 733. Emphasis added.

[5] Marshall Green, John H. Holdridge, and William N. Stokes, *War and Peace with*

This diplomacy rested on three fundamental assumptions. The first was that the confrontation between the West and the Soviet Union would define international relations indefinitely— that the Cold War was a permanent feature of global politics. The second was that the China Mao Zedong had created was stable and would last. Again, into the indefinite future and long after Mao's death, China would fundamentally be a continuation of Maoism under other leaderships. The USSR plus China and the United States would thus form a stable and enduring constellation of three mutually balancing powers and ensure both peace and the interests of the United States. The third and final assumption, as we have seen, was that once the American client state of Taiwan was cut off, its leaders would quickly come to terms with China.

But things did not turn out as Kissinger, Nixon, Mao, and Zhou had confidently expected.

First, the USSR disappeared only a dozen years after President Jimmy Carter had put the final touches on the triangle by decisively cutting off Taiwan.

Second, no sooner had Mao died in 1976 than a coup d'état ousted his chosen successors and brought Deng Xiaoping to power. Deng almost immediately began dismantling Maoist China: Farming was de-collectivized, private trading was made legal, foreign investment and trade were welcomed.

Finally, Taiwan reformed itself, lifting martial law, releasing political prisoners, freeing the press, and carrying out a series of constitutional revisions and elections that abandoned Taipei's claim to rule China while rendering its claim to rule Taiwan absolutely legitimate by every standard of international law.

The existence of this reformed Taiwan, however, and the prospect of its long-term existence had the ironic effect of undermining the stable triangle of power for which Nixon and Carter had aimed. Under the Taiwan Relations Act, the United States

---

China: First-Hand Experiences in the Foreign Service of the United States (Bethesda, Md.: Dacor–Bacon House, 1995), pp. 117–118.

had undertaken major responsibility for the ongoing security of Taiwan. Furthermore, successive Presidents had insisted that nothing would really change for the people of the island. As Jimmy Carter put it, "The United States is confident that the people of Taiwan face a peaceful and prosperous future."[6]

Taiwan's continuing undefined and unrecognized, but real and independent, existence and importance have effectively created a chronic locus for disagreement between China and the United States and other states. Taiwan is of both economic and strategic importance not only to the United States, but also to Japan, Korea, the Philippines, Australia, and many other Pacific nations, which (whatever they may say in public) are deeply worried by China's current military buildup and extensive irredentist territorial claims.

At present, when one leaves Tokyo's Narita Airport heading south, one's flight is handed over to Republic of China air-traffic control in Taipei. Imagine what a disquieting change it would be for the Japanese if, instead, one entered the airspace of the People's Republic of China (PRC). And that, of course, is only a rather small and minor aspect of the tremendous change in the military and strategic structure of East Asia that would follow if Taiwan were actually to join China. Largely unrecognized as it may be, Taiwan is in reality extremely important, probably to be counted among the top five security concerns of the United States and the top three for Japan.

Conflict in the Taiwan Strait would be ruinous for all concerned. As the International Crisis Group in Brussels has assessed the situation:

> An invasion of Taiwan by China cannot be rationally related to two of Beijing's most important objectives: reunification and sustained national economic development. If China did launch such

---

[6]William B. Bader and Jeffrey T. Bergner, eds., *The Taiwan Relations Act: A Decade of Implementation* (Indianapolis: Hudson Institute and SRI International, 1989), p. 159.

an invasion it might well, whatever its ballistic missile capability, lack the military capability to suc-
ceed, particularly if the U.S. intervened, and even
in its best-case scenario, would not be able to sub-
jugate Taiwan without large-scale loss of life. Such
use of force could certainly be expected to lead to
recognition of Taiwan, even an occupied Taiwan,
as an independent sovereign country by major powers such as the U.S. and the EU [European Union].
The subsequent domestic repression in Taiwan
over a protracted period under a China-installed
regime would ensure a total breach between China
and the developed world. Such a breach would
bring a near total end to China's substantial exports
to the developed world and produce massive unemployment in its coastal cities at a time when domestic political stability is under severe strains.[7]

This real importance, however, is not reflected in international usages (although it should be noted that, today in Taipei, there
exist far more "embassies in all but name" than there were actual
embassies in the days when Taipei was more widely recognized).
Thus, on the page in the CIA *World Factbook* for "North Korea,"
one finds the entry: "Official Name: Democratic People's Republic of Korea"—even though Washington does not recognize that
regime. Turning to the page for Taiwan, under "Official Name"
one finds "None," which is simply false, as the state's official name
is "The Republic of China"—a fact of which, arguably, CIA China
analysts and others should probably be aware.[8]

This diplomatic make-believe, irritating as it may be as manifest-
ed in protocol, is genuinely dangerous when it comes to security.

---

[7] "Taiwan Strait II: The Risk of War," *Asia Report*, No. 54 (June 6, 2003).

[8] U.S. Central Intelligence Agency, *The World Factbook 2003*, Brassey's Inc., weekly
updates available at *www.cia.gov/cia/publications/factbook/*. North Korea is at *www.cia.gov/
cia/publications/factbook/geos/kn.html*; for some unknown reason, Taiwan's entry is at the *end*
of the alphabetical listing at *www.cia.gov/cia/publications/factbook/geos/tw.html*.

Until recently, the United States held Taipei at arm's length militarily, even though it was committed to defend the island from attack. The predictable result 25 years later was that Taiwan had "the most isolated military in the world" (as one former Defense Department official put it),[9] was falling behind on technical advances in warfare, and lacked any ability even to communicate with United States forces in the event of war.

Just how dangerous this situation could be was brought home to the Clinton Administration in 1995 and again in 1996, when China fired ballistic missiles near the island in an effort to intimidate voters. It seems that whenever there is a presidential election in Taiwan, the PRC becomes anxious and begins to somehow pressure Washington to ensure that the result is, if not exactly to Beijing's liking, at least acceptable.

Thus, the last time I was involved in a major session about Taiwan was on April 19, 2000, right after the Taiwanese presidential elections. While at the Council on Foreign Relations in New York, I debated with former President Nixon's Chinese interpreter (and later, ambassador to Saudi Arabia for President George H. W. Bush), Charles W. Freeman, Jr.

The atmosphere was rather charged. Freeman explained to a largely sympathetic audience that if the United States did not somehow keep Taiwan under control, it was headed unavoidably for war with China. As Freeman argued:

> There is no longer a credible scenario for peaceful
> reunification. Beijing, not surprisingly, has con-
> cluded that reunification will only be possible
> through coercion. Taiwan and the United States

---

[9] Ed. note: Assistant Secretary of Defense Peter Rodman told the House International Relations Committee that "Taiwan remains isolated, especially in the area of security cooperation. In the international community, the United States stands almost alone in its willingness to assist in the security of Taiwan." See "The Taiwan Relations Act: The Next 25 Years," prepared statement of Peter W. Rodman, Assistant Secretary of Defense for International Security Affairs, before the House International Relations Committee, April 21, 2004, at *http://wwwa.house.gov/international_relations/108/Rod042104.htm.*

are headed toward a violent rendezvous with Chinese nationalism.[10]

I demurred. I did not then believe war was an immediate danger, as Chas did, nor do I now—though that will continue to be true only as long as deterrence is maintained.

Almost exactly a month later, on May 20, 2000, I had the honor of attending the inauguration of Chen Shui-bian as president of the Republic of China. In his inaugural address, among other things, he reached out very clearly to Beijing looking for peace, just as he did when passing through New York City in 2003.

Without in any way dismissing the dangers associated with our relationships with Taiwan and China, or neglecting their promise, I would point out that the fraught debates about them seem to follow the Taiwan electoral cycle. Thus, we have just seen President George W. Bush, with Chinese premier Wen Jiabao standing beside him, reprimand Chen Shui-bian:

> Let me tell you what I've just told the Premier on this issue. The United States government's policy is one China, based upon the three communiqués and the Taiwan Relations Act. We oppose any unilateral decision by either China or Taiwan to change the status quo. And the comments and actions made by the leader of Taiwan indicate that he may be willing to make decisions unilaterally to change the status quo, which we oppose.[11]

This time it was not Ambassador Freeman pushing the panic button, but evidently members of the National Security Council

---

[10] Council on Foreign Relations, "Chas. W. Freeman v. Arthur Waldron: A Debate on China & Taiwan," Meeting at the Council on Foreign Relations, April 19, 2000, at *www.foreignpolicy2000.org/transcripts/t_freeman.html.* Emphasis added.

[11] Office of the White House Press Secretary, "President Bush and Premier Wen Jiabao Remarks to the Press," December 9, 2003, at *www.whitehouse.gov/news/releases/2003/12/20031209-2.html.*

(NSC) and American representatives in Taiwan. President Bush reacted in a confused and inconsistent way—which is perhaps understandable, if not easily forgivable, if one bears in mind the ambiguities, contradictions, and disappointed expectations that for 30 years have defined U.S. policy with respect to Taiwan and China.

So what are we to do? The problem with "Plan A" was, and is, that things did not work out according to it. Washington sought to stabilize the global balance of power; instead, it destabilized the Asian balance of power and, by failing adequately to provide for Taiwan, created a target for constant PRC lobbying.

Had Nixon and Carter possessed greater foresight, there is little doubt that Taiwan could have kept its place in the United Nations and retained some sort of official connection with the United States and a clear international status. At the time, no one considered the need to maintain such aspects of the relationship because they were following the script in which Taiwan disappeared. In the course of establishing relations with China and thereafter, Washington gratuitously abandoned many positions that it could have held, thereby creating the current situation. It is clear that "Plan A" has failed (though some in Washington continue to carry the torch for it), but we lack a "Plan B."

Our present policy seems based on a hope that somehow we can either make "Plan A" work or keep the situation frozen until we figure out what to do. But time and life move inexorably forward. A whole generation has grown up in a Taiwan that has no American embassy and an international profile far smaller than its real importance would require. This population cannot be held in suspended animation forever. Nor is union with China even as plausible today as it was in 2000, when Ambassador Freeman and I debated.

When asked about Hong Kong then, when the system of "one country, two systems" had been in place for three years, Ambassador Freeman noted, "It's alright for the people of Hong Kong to live under the arrangements that have been worked out." Obviously thinking of Hong Kong, he had earlier stated that:

reunification on terms like those proposed by Beijing would threaten no American or allied interest. It would not entail a presence of the People's
Liberation Army in Taiwan. There would be no
change in north-east Asian strategic alliance or balance. It would not alter Taiwan's ability, the ability
of the voters of Taiwan, to elect their own leadership and govern themselves. It would not affect Taiwan's economy or way of life.[12]

That rosy scenario has been completely dispelled by China's
recent crackdown on the democratic movement in Hong Kong.
In effect tearing up the assurances about democracy that it had
made in the Sino–British Joint Declaration of 1984, Beijing is
insisting that it will not allow popular election of Hong Kong's
chief executive and that it will dissolve the Legislative Assembly
should the democratic parties win control. Clearly, the idea that
a democratic Hong Kong could lie down peacefully with a dictatorial China and guide Taiwan back to the "motherland" was a
fantasy. The key assertion in Ambassador Freeman's argument—
that Taiwan could join China yet sustain no damage—has been
disproved by Chinese policy toward Hong Kong.

In Taiwan, as in Hong Kong—where ideas that sounded good
in 1984 have led, on the part of the people of Hong Kong, to
demands for democracy that terrify Beijing—one cannot turn the
clock back. We have to deal with what is really going to happen,
not with what we hoped was going to happen but did not, or with
what we pretend (verbally) is the situation even when our words
are utterly belied by obvious reality. Nor is there any reason to
expect that such change will not occur in China. Nixon and Carter
imagined that the Politburo in Beijing was permanent, whereas
the government in Taipei would disappear. In fact, the opposite
is probably true: An elected president will henceforth govern in
Taipei, but the days of the Politburo are probably numbered.

---

[12] Council on Foreign Relations, "Chas. W. Freeman v. Arthur Waldron."

So what should the United States do? We have, after all, dug ourselves into a very deep verbal and diplomatic hole on the Taiwan issue, guided by false expectations firmly believed. As a result, no simple solution presents itself.

The beginning of wisdom is probably to start acknowledging that "Plan A" *has* failed and begin to engage in what the Chinese call *zhengming* (rectification of names)—that is, calling things what they are, not what we would like them to be. A great deal of leeway exists, even within the cramped and inadequate structures we have imposed on ourselves, for a far more serious involvement with Taiwan than we have had for 30 years. Such involvement is essential today.

Next, it is absolutely vital that we begin to explain to the Chinese that they should perhaps begin to face facts. For example, instead of complaining to Washington about Taiwan and having us relay the message, they should steel themselves and deal directly with Taipei. I am persuaded that a Chinese politician who has the strength and wisdom to acknowledge, stabilize, and make official the current situation (to "baptize the status quo," as it were) would not be lynched by mobs of outraged Chinese nationalists, but rather would be greeted with a great sigh of relief from all concerned (and also with popularity). We should not hector the Chinese or instruct them, but point out the advantages of such a course—which might begin with a reprise of the highly successful 1993 talks in Singapore that have yet to be repeated.

Most important, however, we must see the issues of Taiwan and China against a broader background than is usually provided. China is currently engaged in a vast change, one in which powerful forces of every sort have been unleashed, but one without any clearly stated plan or road map. It is what I have termed a "directionless transition."[13]

At present, Beijing is concerned above all about how to maintain (and even extend) the Communist Party's monopoly on

---

[13] Arthur Waldron, "China's Directionless Transition: A Commentary," *China Brief: A Journal of Information and Analysis*, Vol. IV, No. 4 (February 19, 2004), pp. 4–8. Published by the Jamestown Foundation.

power in an environment of economic and intellectual dynamism, the chief trend of which is not toward continuation of Communist dictatorship, but toward democratization. This problem probably has no answer. Like Communist parties elsewhere, the one in China will sooner or later disappear, swept away by the imperatives of change and the demands of its people. Such change might well lead to a situation in which Taipei's position could be normalized. (It could, of course, also lead to chaos, and hence an even greater need to defend Taiwan.)

The fundamental mistake of "Plan A" China policy as practiced in Washington today is that it mirrors China's concerns. Instead of preparing ourselves for change, we erroneously identify our own interests ever more closely with those of China's rulers—pushed, to a very large degree, by American business. This is unrealistic.

To give one example: The U.S. should clearly support democracy, yet we have been distinctly lukewarm. Why? Because instead of understanding that democratic change may well come to China sooner rather than later—remember that in 1989 the largest pro-democracy demonstrations in human history took place in that country—we are making the sort of mistake we did with the USSR in its last days: identifying not with change, but with a Metternichian sense that it would be best if everything remained the same.

As Edmund Burke wisely noted, "A state without the means of some change is without the means of its conservation."[14] China certainly faces that problem today in nearly every aspect of its economy, society, and governance. The United States faces it as well, as it considers the conundrum of how to design a realistic "Plan B" to replace the "Plan A" that, entrenched as it is in usage and bureaucracy, has so clearly failed.

---

[14] Edmund Burke, *Reflections on the French Revolution & Other Essays* (London: J. M. Dent, Everyman Series, 1912), pp. 19–20.

5

Humoring Chinese Irridentism: Invitation to Disaster?

JOHN J. TKACIK, JR.

L ET ME BEGIN BY POSITING TWO FACTS.

First, by accepting and formally recognizing China's claims to territorial sovereignty over Taiwan, we legitimate China's right to use force against Taiwan whenever it so wishes.

Second, the less Taiwan is accepted into the international community as a full-functioned member able to make significant contributions to the general welfare (that is, the more isolated Taiwan is in the world community), the more likely communist China is to use force to threaten or attack democratic Taiwan.

From these two postulates, it seems to me that a "one China" policy makes war in the Taiwan Strait—or the ultimate intimidation of democratic Taiwan to surrender to the demands of communist China—more likely.

What "One China" Does *Not* Do

For many years I argued that America's "one China" policy had been useful because of the two things it does *not* do: It does not

This contribution is an adaptation of remarks prepared for a symposium, "Rethinking 'One China': A Fiction More Dangerous Than Useful?" held at The Heritage Foundation on February 26, 2004.

recognize China's claims to Taiwan and it does not make China angry. Never in the past century has the United States recognized Chinese sovereignty over Taiwan, and consequently the United States has steadfastly maintained the position (although American leaders have never said so publicly) that China has no right in international law or otherwise to use, or threaten the use of, force against Taiwan.

The legal position of the United States on the matter of sovereignty over Taiwan is that:

> Article 2 of the Japanese Peace treaty, signed on September 8, 1951 at San Francisco, provides that "Japan renounces all right, title and claim to Formosa and the Pescadores." The same language was used in Article 2 of the Treaty of Peace between China and Japan signed on April 28, 1952. In neither treaty did Japan cede this area to any particular entity. As Taiwan and the Pescadores are not covered by any existing international disposition, *sovereignty over the area is an unsettled question subject to future international resolution.* Both the Republic of China and the Chinese Communists disagree with this conclusion and consider that Taiwan and the Pescadores are part of the sovereign state of China. The United States recognized the Government of the Republic of China as legitimately occupying and exercising jurisdiction over Taiwan and the Pescadores.[1]

An extensive history of this legal position is encompassed in a memorandum entitled "Legal Status of Taiwan."[2] It is important to understand that this remains the position of the United States. On July 14, 1982, President Ronald Reagan sent a letter to Taiwan's

---

[1] U.S. Senate, Committee on Foreign Relations, *Part IV (Republic of China): Hearing Before the Subcommittee on the United States Security Agreements and Commitments Abroad,* 91st Cong., 2nd Sess., 1970, p. 948. Emphasis added.

[2] U.S. Department of State, Office of the Legal Advisor to the Director of Republic of China Affairs, "Legal Status of Taiwan," July 13, 1971. Reproduced as Appendix C of this

President Chiang Ching-kuo, which reassured him that, among other things, "the United States had not altered its position regarding sovereignty over Taiwan."[3] This was a legal position to which even the exile-government of the Republic of China based in Taipei seemed resigned.

In July 1952, Republic of China Foreign Minister George Yeh told the Legislative Yuan in Taipei that under the San Francisco Peace Treaty, "no provision was made for the return [of these islands] to China." He continued:

> Formosa and the Pescadores were formerly Chinese territories. As Japan has renounced her claim to Formosa and the Pescadores, only China has the right to take them over. In fact, we are controlling them now, and undoubtedly they constitute a part of our territories. However, the delicate international situation makes it that they do not belong to us. Under present circumstances, Japan has no right to transfer Formosa and the Pescadores to us; nor can we accept such a transfer from Japan even if she so wishes....[4]

The Core Concept

Although China breathes fire at the mere thought that "the status of Taiwan remains undetermined," that concept is at the core of America's commitment to the survival and success of democracy in Taiwan.

In 1976, Secretary of State Henry Kissinger asked his top China aides: "If Taiwan is recognized by us as part of China, then

---

volume. The original document is housed at the National Archives and Records Administration, in retired State Department files for the Office of Republic of China Affairs (EAP/ROC) in the POL–19 TAIWAN file. This document was declassified on September 7, 1996.

[3]John H. Holdridge, *Crossing the Divide: An Insider's Account of Normalization of U.S.–China Relations* (Lanham, Md.: Rowan and Littlefield, 1997), pp. 184–185.

[4]"Legal Status of Taiwan," July 13, 1971.

it may become irresistible to them. Our saying we want a peaceful solution has no force: it is Chinese territory. What are we going to do about it?"[5] Arthur Hummel, then Assistant Secretary of State and later ambassador to Beijing, responded, "Down the road, perhaps the only solution would be an independent Taiwan."[6]

Those were the days when diplomats actually understood what a "one China" policy would mean. Secretary Kissinger realized that to recognize Taiwan as a part of China would legitimize China's threats to use force against the island. When Ambassador Leonard Woodcock negotiated normalization with Deng Xiaoping in December 1978, he had to assure Deng that the United States would not recognize both the People's Republic of China and the Republic of China. Hence, America's "one China" policy. It did not mean that we recognized that Taiwan was thenceforth under Chinese sovereignty; it meant merely that the government of the United States recognized only one government of China at a time.

Since the 1920s, before the invention of the term "one China," the phrase "China's territorial integrity" had been a diplomatic code word for an agreement among the Western powers (and Japan) not to dismember China into autonomous baronies, which could be dominated by individual colonial powers. The United States insisted that its policy was to preserve the "territorial integrity" of one China in order to prevent other powers from carving up the country. This policy prevented the United States from recognizing the Japanese puppet state of Manchukuo.

That, however, is *all* that was meant by "China's territorial integrity," not that, somehow, every territory that had ever been under Chinese sovereignty would be returned to Chinese sovereignty.

With the death of Generalissimo Chiang Kai-shek's son in January 1988, the government of the Republic of China was basically without even the traditional legitimacy of dynastic succession. New President Lee Teng-hui immediately sought to construct a

---

[5] William Burr, ed., *The Kissinger Transcripts: The Top Secret Talks with Beijing and Moscow* (New York: New Press, 1999), p 464.

[6] *Ibid.*

new foundation of legitimacy for the ROC by restructuring the Legislative Yuan and the National Assembly into parliamentary bodies that truly represented the Taiwanese people. But the new president also knew that the ROC could not sustain its own legitimacy if it persisted in its claim to be the sovereign authority over the Chinese mainland, much less over independent Mongolia.

In November 1993, President Bill Clinton, under pressure from Beijing, disinvited Taiwan's President Lee Teng-hui from the Asia Pacific Economic Cooperation (APEC) forum "chief executives" summit—despite the fact that APEC bylaws mandated that all "member economies" be treated equally. President Lee then began a campaign to identify Taiwan as separate from China. At the summit, President Lee's personal representative, P.K. Chiang, read a statement proclaiming Taiwan's "Interim Two-China's Policy," which declared that "[t]he term 'China' has distinct geographical, historical and cultural connotations, and within 'China' there are two independent, sovereign and mutually non-subordinate nations."[7]

China's Military Modernization and Taiwan

Since the collapse of the Soviet Union, China has pursued a course of military modernization focused primarily on Taiwan, justifying vast expenditures on advanced weaponry in an effort to deter American involvement in a Taiwan Strait crisis. In 1995 and 1996, after the United States repeatedly assured China that it pursued a "one China" policy, China launched mock missile attacks in the Taiwan Strait; all civilian maritime and aviation traffic was halted in that heavily traveled sea lane for days.

In 1995, the State Department response was that the missile strikes "did not contribute to peace and stability in the region." Emboldened, the next Chinese missile attack struck closer to Taiwan's territory, obliging the United States to take more forceful action: It dispatched two U.S. Navy carrier battle groups to the

---

[7] "Economic Minister Refutes Jiang Zemin's One-China Speech," Taipei China Broadcasting Corp. News Services, Hookup program (in Mandarin), November 21, 1993, transcribed by BBC at 212300 CE/Badgley DB052211.003 MY 22/0751Z NOV.

Strait. Regrettably, even as late as December 2003, the State
Department reaction to China's missile buildup on the Taiwan
Strait was to state, "We have felt that missile deployments are not
conducive to a dialogue."[8]

Reacting to President George W. Bush's statements in December 2003 relating to moves by Taiwan's president to hold a referendum designed to protest China's missile threat to this country,
Chinese premier Wen Jiabao seems to have gotten the impression that President Bush was "against Taiwan independence." In
December 2003, shortly after Wen Jiabao had visited Washington, analyst Willy Lam quoted a Politburo member as saying:

> If Chen Shui-bian were to disturb the status quo
> via holding referendums and other means, *and we
> were to respond militarily*, the U.S. can't raise objec-
> tions let alone interfere, after all, Bush has already
> indicated unambiguous opposition to attempts by
> Taipei to change the status quo.[9]

Next, consider remarks made by Deputy Secretary of State
Richard Armitage in Beijing on January 30, 2004:

> The fact of the matter is, it's now twenty five years
> since we normalized relations, this year, and the
> question of Taiwan has been handled sensitively
> and sensibly by I used to say successive govern-
> ments, but now I can say successive generations
> both in the U.S. and in the People's Republic of
> China, and we look for that wisdom to continue.[10]

---

[8] Transcript of Department of State Daily Press Briefing, Richard Boucher, Briefer,
December 16, 2003, at *www.state.gov/r/pa/prs/dpb/2003/27327.htm.*

[9] Willy Wo-Lap Lam, "China Claims a Big Win over Taiwan," CNN.COM, December 15,
2003, at *http://edition.cnn.com/2003/WORLD/asiapcf/east/12/15/willy.column/index.html*
(December 17, 2003). Emphasis added.

[10] Transcript of "Media Round Table, Richard L. Armitage, Deputy Secretary of State,
Beijing, China, January 30, 2004, at *www.state.gov/s/d/rm/28614.htm.*

Finally, from the presidential campaign trail, Senator John Kerry (D–MA) commented about our "one China" policy:

> [T]he United States has always had a one China policy, notwithstanding how terrible we may understand their regime to be. And that has been a Republican president, Democrat president policy alike. I think it is the right policy. I think now is the time for us to also be strong with Taiwan and to make it clear that while we are supportive of the democracy, and while we recognize the society they've built in a capitalist society, we are not going to permit them to declare independence; that would be unacceptable. And I think the way we resolve it is to continue to push, as we did with Hong Kong, Macao and other places, for a "one China, two systems," and work through over the course of the future.[11]

This is truly frightening. A top Republican Administration diplomat characterizes China's handling of the Taiwan question over the past 25 years as "sensitive and sensible," and a man who has spent much of his Senate career as either the chairman or the ranking minority member of the Asian Affairs Subcommittee, and who could conceivably be elected President, declares that the United States should "resolve" the Taiwan issue by continuing to push for a "one China, two systems" formula "as we did with Hong Kong [and] Macao."

This is why the words "one China" have ceased to be useful (if they ever were) as a description of American policy and are instead becoming dangerous. "One country, two systems" is Beijing's formula, not ours; Beijing foisted it upon Hong Kong, not

---

[11] See Transcript of National Public Radio Democratic Presidential Candidates Debate, January 6, 2004, at *www.vote-smart.org/debate_transcripts/trans_29.pdf*. See also "Democrat Primaries Candidate Blasts Bush Attitude Toward Taiwan," Taipei Central News Agency, January 7, 2004.

us. Yet responsible elected representatives and intelligent diplomats have adopted China's meaning of the phrase "one China" in place of our own.

Why is that? Because America's "one China" policy does not mean "one China."

What Does "One China" Really Mean?

Just what is *our* "one China" policy? Deputy Assistant Secretary of State for East Asian and Pacific Affairs Randall G. Schriver described it—after a fashion:

[W]e maintain our one-China policy, *our one-China policy,* as defined by:

— the three joint communiqués and
— the Taiwan Relations Act.

There are other elements that support this policy, such as

— our strong opposition to the use of force,
— our non-support for Taiwan independence, and
— our support for the six assurances.[12]

None of these elements of U.S. policy, however, commits the United States to a position on the matter of sovereignty with respect to Taiwan. The three "Joint Communiqués" go out of their way to avoid the issue of whether the United States itself believes that Taiwan is part of China.

- The Shanghai Communiqué danced around the subject: "The United States acknowledges that all Chinese on either side of the Taiwan Strait maintain there is but one China and that Taiwan is a part of China. The

---

[12] *Hearing on Military Modernization and Cross-Strait Balance,* U.S.–China Economic and Security Review Commission, 108th Cong., 2nd Sess., February 6, 2004, p.13, at *www.uscc.gov/hearings/2004hearings/transcripts/04_02_06.pdf.* Emphasis added.

> United States Government does not challenge that position."[13]

- The Normalization Communiqué simply "acknowledges the *Chinese* position that there is but one China and Taiwan is part of China."[14] When questioned on this point during hearings on the Taiwan Relations Act of 1979, the Carter Administration agreed that it had acknowledged the "Chinese position" that Taiwan is part of China but emphasized that "the United States has *not* itself agreed to this position."[15]

- The August 17, 1982, Communiqué was premised on President Reagan's accompanying statement that "The Taiwan question is a matter for the Chinese people, on both sides of the Taiwan Strait, to resolve. We will not interfere in this matter or prejudice the free choice of, or put pressure on, the people of Taiwan in this matter."[16]

Next in Secretary Schriver's canon of "our one-China policy" is the Taiwan Relations Act, signed by President Carter on April 10, 1979. Section 4(b)(1) of the Taiwan Relations Act states that "[w]henever the laws of the United States refer or relate to foreign countries, nations, states, governments, or similar entities, such terms shall include and such laws shall apply with respect to Taiwan."[17]

---

[13] "Joint Communique of the United States of America and the People's Republic of China, February 28, 1972," also known as the "Shanghai Communiqué." A version is available at the United States Embassy in Beijing Web site at *www.usembassy-china. org.cn/irc/policy/jtcomm1.html*.

[14] Known as the "Normalization Communique" of December 16, 1978, a version is available at the United States Embassy in Beijing Web site at *www.usembassy-china. org.cn/irc/policy/jtcomm1.html*.

[15] Senate Report 96–7, *Taiwan Enabling Act Conference Report, Report of the Committee on Foreign Relations, United States Senate, Together with Additional Views on S. 245*, March 1, 1979, p. 7. Emphasis in original.

[16] See Presidential Statement on Issuance of Communique, August 17, 1982, in hearing, *China–Taiwan: United States Policy*, Committee on Foreign Affairs, U.S. House of Representatives, 97th Cong., 2nd Sess., August 18, 1982, p. 33.

[17] Taiwan Relations Act, Public Law 96–8, Section 4(b)(b)(1), April 10, 1979.

Section 15 (2) defines the term Taiwan as including, "as the context may require,"

> the islands of Taiwan and the Pescadores, the people
> on those islands, corporations and other entities and
> associations created or organized under the laws
> applied on those islands, and the governing authori-
> ties on Taiwan recognized by the United States as the
> *Republic of China* prior to January 1, 1979, and *any*
> *successor governing authorities* (including political sub-
> divisions, agencies, and instrumentalities thereof).[18]

Perhaps most important in the context of "one China" was Secretary Schriver's inclusion of President Reagan's "Six Assurances" to Taiwan's president on July 14, 1982. They were:

— The United States would not set a date for ending arms
  sales to Taiwan;
— The United States would not hold prior consultations
  with the Chinese on arms sales to Taiwan;
— The United States would not play any mediation role
  between Taiwan and Beijing;
— The United States had not agreed to revise the Taiwan
  Relations Act;
— *The United States had not altered its position regarding sov-*
  ereignty over Taiwan; and
— The United States would not exert pressure on Taiwan
  to enter into negotiations with the Chinese.[19]

Conclusion

Under domestic law, the United States treats Taiwan, whether under the name "Republic of China" or the name of "any successor

---

[18] Taiwan Relations Act, Section 15(2). Emphasis added.

[19] See Holdridge, statement to House Foreign Affairs Committee in *China–Taiwan: United States Policy*, pp. 16–17. Emphasis added.

governing authorities," as a foreign country independent of China. For defense purposes, domestic law grants Taiwan the same status as a "major non-NATO ally."[20] For diplomatic purposes, the United States does not recognize China's claims to sovereignty over the island and no U.S. laws requiring diplomatic ties or formal recognition apply with respect to Taiwan.[21]

Over the years, however, America's "one China" policy—unexplicated and unqualified—has given both Chinese leaders and leading American politicians the impression that we consider democratic Taiwan to be a part of communist China. "One China," then, is no longer a convenient legal fiction designed to help Beijing keep face. It is the acquiescence in China's *casus belli* against Taiwan. As such, it only legitimizes China's threats to use force against Taiwan and, if unanswered, encourages China to believe that the United States will not defend Taiwan's democracy.

In 1933, the United States signed the Montevideo Convention on Rights and Duties of States, which defines independent states in the following way:

> ARTICLE 1: The state as a person of international law should possess the following qualifications: a) a permanent population; b) a defined territory; c) government; and d) capacity to enter into relations with the other states....

> ARTICLE 3: The *political existence of the state is independent of recognition by the other states.* Even before recognition the state has the right to defend its integrity and independence....

---

[20] For example, Taiwan is treated as a "major non-NATO ally" in such legislation as the Universal Jurisdiction Rejection Act of 2003 (H. R. 2050). passed during the first session of the 108th Congress.

[21] Section 4(b)(8) of the TRA states: "No requirement, whether expressed or implied, under the laws of the United States with respect to the maintenance of diplomatic relations or recognition shall be applicable with respect to Taiwan."

ARTICLE 4: States are juridically equal, enjoy the
same rights, and have equal capacity in their exercise. The rights of each one do not depend upon
the power which it possesses to assure its exercise,
but upon the simple fact of its existence as a person under international law.[22]

Given (1) that Taiwan's government is seen by all of its own
people as the legitimate and sovereign government of Taiwan,
(2) that Taiwan has now developed into Asia's most vibrant and
dynamic democracy, (3) that the United States has never accepted the People's Republic of China's claims to sovereignty over
Taiwan, and (4) that Taiwan meets all the qualifications of an
independent state under international law, it is clear that maintaining an unqualified "one China" policy only weakens America's commitment to the global expansion of democracy and
encourages China to believe that America will eventually abandon its commitment to Taiwan.

The "one China" policy therefore makes Chinese miscalcula-
tion more likely, makes war more likely, and undermines America's leadership among the democracies of the Asia–Pacific
Region.

---

[22] Convention on Rights and Duties of States (Inter-American), December 26, 1933, 49
Stat. 3097, Treaty Series 881, at *www.yale.edu/lawweb/avalon/intdip/interam/intamo3.htm#art3*.
Emphasis added. Convention signed at Montevideo; Senate advice and consent to ratification, with a reservation, June 15, 1934; ratified by the President of the United States, with a
reservation, June 29, 1934; ratification of the United States deposited with the Pan American Union July 13, 1934; entered into force December 26, 1934; proclaimed by the President of the United States January 18, 1935; Article 8 reaffirmed by protocol of December
23, 1936.

6

Cognitive Dissonance: China and the Bush Doctrine

THOMAS DONNELLY

NATIONAL SECURITY STRATEGIES ARE LIKE SNAKESKINS: GOOD for one season but best shed to allow for new growth. So it is with the outgrown "one China" policy. Once supple and smooth, it is now a dry crust that chafes and irritates, a scab on healthy American strategy-making.

The United States has had a particularly difficult time shedding its Cold War skins. For more than a decade after the fall of the Berlin Wall and the collapse of the Soviet empire, partisans and analysts of all stripes devoted most of their effort to trying to repair the rotting flesh of the strategies and policies of the past.

The attacks of September 11, 2001, awoke Americans to the fact that the world was still a dangerous place—that neither "assertive multilateralism" nor balance-of-power realism could serve the nation in a new century. But a coherent strategy is more than a renewal of will or the "transformation" of military might. Moreover, a global superpower in an increasingly "globalized"

This contribution is an adaptation of remarks prepared for a symposium "Rethinking 'One China': A Fiction More Dangerous Than Useful?" held at The Heritage Foundation on February 26, 2004.

world must make global strategy; a disconnected, region-by-region approach is likely to be self-defeating.

Thus, we must recognize that the so-called Bush Doctrine is still very much a work in progress. It has within it what might be termed the genetic code for a lithe and muscular, healthy global strategy, but the process of regeneration is incomplete. Its great weakness is its failure to apply its most basic tenets to East Asia, to China and Taiwan, and to recognize the centrality of the standoff across the Taiwan Strait to the regional and, indeed, the long-term global balance of power. As the Fulda Gap was to the Cold War, so the Taiwan Strait is to the emerging international system of the 21st century.

Before the Bush Doctrine

As noted above, the new national security strategy of the United States is still being developed. But for the attacks of 9/11, George W. Bush would almost certainly have followed the uncertain, post–Cold War drift of his father and his predecessor. We should recall that, in the 2000 campaign, candidate Bush constantly excoriated Al Gore for the promiscuous use of U.S. military forces in open-ended "nation-building" missions, squandering American strength to no real strategic purpose. Surrounding himself with a group of extraordinarily seasoned statesmen—self-described "Vulcans" of the policymaking establishment—the President vowed to restore a sense of realism to the Oval Office.

In his first year in office, President Bush made good on this promise. This was perhaps most notable in the first crisis of his presidency, when on April 1, 2001, a hot-rodding Chinese interceptor bumped into a U.S. EP–3 surveillance plane, causing the Chinese pilot to lose control of his aircraft and crash and the American plane to make an emergency landing on Hainan Island. It would be hard to dream up a clearer case of Chinese provocation short of actually firing upon U.S. forces.

The one element of potentially new thinking in Bush rhetoric to that point—acknowledging the People's Republic as a "strategic competitor" rather than as a "strategic partner," as the Clinton Administration had claimed—was tossed immediately and unceremoniously out the window: no hobgoblins of foolish consistency for the Vulcans. A White House spokesman made it clear that the Administration did not want to "overreact" to the situation. "We wanted to give the Chinese time, to avoid an escalation," said a Bush spokesperson. The President himself said only that China's delay in allowing American access to the EP–3 crew was "inconsistent with standard diplomatic practice and with the expressed desire of both our countries for better relations."[1]

The longer the incident went unresolved, the more humiliating the crisis became. The Chinese were immediately truculent about returning the EP–3, with state television declaring that "the U.S. has total responsibility for the event."[2] In the end, on the recommendation of Secretary of State Colin Powell, who had shoved aside the Pentagon to seize control of the crisis, President Bush would only say, "This has been a difficult situation for both our countries. I know that the American people join me in expressing sorrow for the loss of life of a Chinese pilot."[3]

Though pleased by the resolution of the crisis, U.S. Sinologists immediately argued that peace had been saved by Chinese leader Jiang Zemin, who now deserved special consideration. As a State Department official put it, "In the Chinese view, Jiang went way out there to get the crew back." American assertiveness, especially American ties to Taiwan including arms sales, would "undercut" Jiang, "to put it mildly."[4]

Alas, President Bush did not feel the same sense of debt to the Chinese leader. Just three weeks later, in a television interview, the President declared that the United States would do "whatever it took" to defend Taiwan, indeed saying that the defense of the island was an American "obligation."

---

[1] Steven Mufson and Philip P. Pan, "Spy Plane Delays Irk President; Bush Asks 'Prompt' Release by Chinese," *The Washington Post*, April 3, 2001, p. A1.

[2] Elisabeth Rosenthal and David E. Sanger, "U.S. Plane in China After It Collides with Chinese Jet," *The New York Times*, April 2, 2001, p. A1.

[3] David E. Sanger and Steven Lee Myers, "Collision with China: Delicate Diplomatic Dance Ends Bush's First Crisis," *The New York Times*, April 11, 2001, p. A1.

[4] *Ibid.*

Such clarity shocked the acolytes of "strategic ambiguity." Massachusetts Senator John Kerry took to the microphones to charge that the "implications" of the change were "serious" and "serve[d] neither our interest nor Taiwan's." He was reluctant to commit to the defense of Taiwan because he "understood the danger of doing so." If he did, Kerry acted as though he had never fully thought through the possibility of facing such a crisis: "[I]f China attacked in response to what it sees as a Taiwanese provocation would we then respond? Apparently so...."[5]

To be fair, there was meant to be a method to the maddening inconsistencies of early Bush Administration policy: Realist strategy-making prizes freedom of action above all else, and national interests above ideology. Bred to build a balance of power and deeply suspicious of moral claims in international politics, the mini-Metternichs among America's foreign policy mandarins have been more than happy to create uncertainty about U.S. intentions.

This has been nowhere more true than in regard to China strategy, which was designed to create ambiguity rather than clarity. The fact that the "one China" policy rests on an obvious fiction is a plus-factor in the conventional wisdom of American strategists.

The Bush Doctrine, Properly Understood

The attacks of September 11, 2001, destroyed not only the twin World Trade Center towers and a facade of the Pentagon, but also the conventional wisdom of post–Cold War U.S. security policy. Al-Qaeda and the Taliban were forces not amenable to American balancing-from-a-distance: They were, rather, ideological and violent organizations dedicated to making war on the United States and killing Americans wherever they could be struck.

But though this war had been going on for years prior to 9/11, and though President Bush instantly intuited this fact, the initial reaction of the State Department, for example, was to negotiate

[5] U.S. Department of State, International Information Programs, "Text: Kerry Says U.S. Not Obligated to Defend Taiwan from Attacks (Sen. Kerry's speech on President Bush's remarks)," April 25, 2001, at *http://usinfo.org/USIA/usinfo.state.gov/regional/ea/uschina/taikerry.htm*.

with the Taliban to turn over Osama bin Laden. Indeed, the Democratic Party still has not fully accepted that the United States is at war.

In the course of the year following September 11, the President gradually fleshed out a larger response to the new realities. Importantly, the problem of terrorism from the first was linked to the larger political problems of the greater Middle East and "rogue regimes"—the "Axis of Evil." It was also rightly linked to the dangers of nuclear proliferation and, ultimately, to the cause of political liberty in the world.

Equally important, President Bush understood that American strength—especially U.S. military strength—was the most effective means for responding to these present dangers. Operations Enduring Freedom and Iraqi Freedom are now clearly part of a "generational commitment" (Condoleezza Rice's term) to transforming not only Iraq and Afghanistan, but also the rotten political order in the greater Middle East. The goal is not simply to contain the region's threats, but to "roll back" the forms of autocracy from which the threats emanate.

The September 2002 *National Security Strategy of the United States*[6] was the first attempt to articulate a comprehensive "forward strategy of freedom." Yet, in the political context of the time (the beginning of the run-up to the Iraq war), there was a question whether the new strategy was simply a rationalization for removing the regime of Saddam Hussein or whether a war in Iraq would be the first exemplar of a fundamental and lasting shift in American strategic thought. What makes this an open question still is uncertainty about the Administration's stance toward the long-awaited rise of China.

The basic argument of the Bush Doctrine is that the United States must maintain its role as "sole superpower"—the global guarantor of a stable, liberal democratic order—in order to preserve peace and expand liberty in the 21st century. Among the

---

[6] U.S. National Security Council, *The National Security Strategy of the United States of America*, September 2002, at *www.whitehouse.gov/nsc/nss.html.* Cited hereafter as *NSS.*

key implications of this doctrine are that Americans retain the
political will and military strength to keep the great-power peace
in Europe, the greater Middle East, and East Asia while preventing rogue regimes and terrorists from acquiring the ability (particularly through the development or purchase of nuclear arms)
to upset the post–Cold War *Pax Americana.*

This is not an unreasonable hope: The United States runs no
immediate risk of the "imperial overstretch" that is supposed to
be (in the realist account, at least) the inevitable downfall of great
powers. The other large and wealthy nations of the world are all
at least nominally America's allies. As William Wohlforth has con-
vincingly argued, the so-called unipolar moment is uniquely
peaceful, stable, and durable.[7] Since the fall of the Soviet Union,
the prospect for major war in Europe has been nearly unimagin-
able; the Balkans wars of the 1990s were remarkable for the fact
that, by contrast to 1914, they could not generate a great-power
conflict.

While it is impossible within the scope of this essay to make
the complete case for eventual success in the project of Middle
East "transformation"—and it is necessary to understand the
effort as a "long, hard slog," in Defense Secretary Donald Rumsfeld's blunt assessment—the quick military victories in
Afghanistan and Iraq suggest that America's enemies, though
numerous, are individually weak. As Libya's decision to end its
nuclear program indicates, the region has begun to accommo-
date the expanding U.S. direct role.

A China Exception?

When it comes to China, however, there is a distinct gap
between the rhetoric of the Bush Doctrine and the reality of Bush
policy. Indeed, disturbingly, China policy seems to be the last
redoubt of the conventional-wisdom crowd.

---

[7] See William C. Wohlforth, "The Stability of a Unipolar World," *The MIT Press Jour-
nals,* no date, at *http://mitpress.mit.edu/journals/pdf/isec_24_01_5_0.pdf.* The term "unipolar moment" was coined by Charles Krauthammer. See Charles Krauthammer, "The
Unipolar Moment," *Foreign Affairs,* Vol. 70, No. 1 (Winter 1990/1991), pp. 23–33.

The discussion of China in the National Security Strategy leaves a lot of room for doubt about how hard the United States will push for change in Beijing:

> A quarter century after beginning the process of shedding the worst features of the Communist legacy, China's leaders have not yet made the next series of fundamental choices about the character of their state…. In time, China will find that social and political freedom is the only source of [national] greatness.[8]

While appearing strong, such language echoes the empty hope that political liberalization is an inevitable consequence of economic development. In fact, the entire premise of China's drive for "modernization" is exactly the opposite.

The pattern of Administration diplomacy seems to have returned to the strategic ambiguities of the past. Since 9/11, Beijing has been warmly embraced for its supposed contributions to the global war on terrorism. But as John Tkacik of The Heritage Foundation has persuasively argued, there is precious little that the People's Republic has done to aid the fight against al-Qaeda; Beijing's main contribution has been to step up the repression of the Uighurs in western China, probably accelerating the radicalization of a Muslim people whose culture and society is under siege by the forced resettlement of Han Chinese in Xinjiang province.[9]

Moreover, lest we forget, China was a staunch, if quiet, ally to France in opposing a U.N. resolution backing the removal of Saddam Hussein from Iraq.[10] The uncovering of the A.Q. Khan

---

[8] *NSS*, p. 27.

[9] John J. Tkacik, Jr., "Time for Washington to Take a Realistic Look at China Policy," Heritage Foundation *Backgrounder* No. 1717, December 22, 2003, at *www.heritage.org/ Research/AsiaandthePacific/bg1717.cfm*.

[10] John Tkacik and Nile Gardiner, "China Will 'Stand Aside' on Iraq," *Asian Wall Street Journal*, February 10, 2003, at *http://online.wsj.com/article/0,,SB104482784888205294 3,00.html*.

proliferation scandal in Pakistan is revealing Beijing's role in making the world's most dangerous weapons increasingly available to the world's most dangerous regimes and, frighteningly, to terrorist groups.[11] Many parts of the "Islamic Bomb" should have a "Made in China" label stenciled on them. The best one can say about the PRC's performance since 9/11 is that they kept mum while U.S. forces moved into Central Asian bases to invade Afghanistan.

In typical fashion, the Bush Administration has seized upon the change of Chinese leadership from Jiang Zemin to Hu Jintao as the moment to embark upon one of the periodic "improve the relationship" offensives that Americans seem unable to resist. As Robert Kagan has written, for American China analysts, "the relationship" is regarded as an end in itself rather than as a means to achieve American political or strategic goals. Even Henry Kissinger, the original architect of current China policy, prided himself on rejecting this view of professional Sinologists.[12]

Thus, there has arisen, as Ellen Bork has put it, a "China exception" to the Bush Doctrine.[13] In his widely hailed November 6, 2003, speech to the National Endowment for Democracy, in which he admitted that American support for autocratic regimes in the Middle East had advanced neither the cause of liberty nor U.S. national security interests, the President would only allow that "eventually" the Chinese people would "want their liberty pure and whole."[14] At the same time, Secretary of State Colin Powell was giving a speech at Texas A&M University claiming that

---

[11] Joby Warrick and Peter Slevin, "Libyan Arms Designs Traced Back to China, Pakistanis Resold Chinese-Provided Plans," *The Washington Post,* February 15, 2004, p. A1, at *www.washingtonpost.com/wp-dyn/articles/A42692–2004Feb14.html.*

[12] Robert Kagan, "U.S. Policy Toward Taiwan: Creating a New Reality," undated manuscript, courtesy of the Project for the New American Century, p. 2.

[13] Ellen Bork, "No Exceptions for Democracy in China," *The Washington Post,* November 15, 2003, p. A23, at *www.washingtonpost.com/ac2/wp-dyn/A43054–2003Nov14.*

[14] Office of the White House Press Secretary, "President Bush Discusses Freedom in Iraq and Middle East: (Remarks by the President at the 20th Anniversary of the National Endowment for Democracy, United States Chamber of Commerce)," November 6, 2003, at *www.whitehouse.gov/news/releases/2003/11/20031106–2.html.*

China acts "in cooperation with us, not in competition with us....
[This] is how real friends get along."[15]

And when, a month later, Chinese premier Wen Jiabao visited
Washington, officials at the National Security Council and elsewhere in the bureaucracy cooked up a scheme to have President
Bush make amends for his 2001 promise to defend Taiwan. The
week before Wen's December 2003 visit, Chinese military officers
warned that Taiwan faced an "abyss of war" if it persisted in holding a referendum the following spring demanding that China
reverse the buildup of missile and other military forces across the
Taiwan Strait. (The controversial referendum was indeed included on the March 20, 2004, ballot, but it failed due to low voter
participation.) Parroting the Chinese line that the referendum
was not simply an attempt to address a military threat but actually
a move toward independence for Taiwan, President Bush
deplored "the comments and actions made by" Taiwanese President Chen Shui-bian, which allegedly "indicate that he may be
willing to make decisions unilaterally to change the status quo."[16]

Somehow, the perverse view persists that Taipei—prosperous,
truly, even fractiously democratic, the strategic linchpin of East
Asia and the most potent symbol of the United States' ability to
guarantee the safety of its allies even in the face of a Communist
colossus—rather than Beijing is the problem. In a recent issue of
Foreign Affairs, longtime China watcher Michael Swaine expresses
precisely this attitude. He is unimpressed by China's military
buildup across the Strait: It is not a "new threat" and "do[es] not
constitute clear evidence that Beijing actually intends to attack
the island."[17] One wonders what he thinks the missiles were doing
there and why the Chinese are adding more as fast as they can—

---

[15] Colin L. Powell, "Remarks at Conference on China–U.S. Relations," November 5,
2003, at *www.state.gov/secretary/rm/2003/25950.htm.*

[16] Office of the White House Press Secretary, "Remarks by President Bush and Premier
Wen Jiabao in Photo Opportunity," December 9, 2003, at *www.whitehouse.gov/news/releases/
2003/12/20031209-2.html.* See also William Kristol, Robert Kagan, and Gary Schmitt,
"U.S.–China–Taiwan Policy," Project for the New American Century, December 9, 2003.

[17] Michael D. Swaine, "Trouble in Taiwan," *Foreign Affairs,* March/April 2004, at
www.foreignaffairs.org/20040301faessay83205/michael-d-swaine/trouble-in-taiwan/html.

although it is true that the missiles' intimidation value is greater than their strict tactical value.

"One China" and the Bush Doctrine

To preserve the "one China" policy contradicts the two most fundamental tenets of the Bush Doctrine: the assertion of universal political rights and the need for American primacy. Why should the liberation of Beijing be less urgent than the liberation of Baghdad? This is not to recommend an invasion of mainland China, but it is to recognize that "eventual" freedom is no substitute for actual freedom.

Finally, the United States has a compelling national security interest in preventing the "unification" of China with Taiwan. President Bush committed the ultimate gaffe—telling the truth—when he admitted that America would do what it takes to defend Taiwan. "Strategic ambiguity" has, in fact, been a dead letter since the crises of 1995 and 1996, when the Clinton Administration was forced to respond to the Chinese "missile blockade" of Taiwan:

> [W]hen China began aggressive military intimidation of Taiwan, for the United States the issue immediately transcended Taiwan. Even though there was not even a real prospect Taiwan would be invaded, with whatever strategic consequences that might entail, the U.S. administration believed it could not stand back and allow Taiwan to be intimidated by the Chinese military. American credibility was at stake, and American officials, especially in the Pentagon, felt this viscerally. East Asian allies were watching for signs of American timidity. Their fear that China was prepared to use military force and intimidation to have its way, undeterred by the United States, raised immediate questions about the future of U.S. staying power in East Asia.[18]

---

[18] Kagan, "U.S. Policy Toward Taiwan: Creating a New Reality," p. 9.

Not only East Asia, but also the rest of the world is watching how the United States reacts to the continued rise of China. Moreover, China is watching how well the United States fulfills its role of global leadership.

This is especially true in the greater Middle East; the Islamic world extends into Central, South, and Southeast Asia, directly abutting Chinese interests. The rise of China is not only a regional challenge, but a global challenge as well. Rapid Chinese growth has made Beijing an increasing consumer of Persian Gulf energy. The PRC's export-driven economy has benefited from globalization, but this also sparks global political and security interests.

It is an exaggeration to assert that for want of a Taiwanese nail, the American kingdom might be lost, but it is true that a failure to peacefully contain Chinese ambitions (which begin at the shores of the Taiwan Strait) will make the new American century much shorter and the "empire of liberty" much smaller. Shedding the moldering skin of "one China" is long overdue.

7

Two Congressmen Look at "One China"

THE HONORABLE ROBERT E. ANDREWS
AND THE HONORABLE STEVE CHABOT

REPRESENTATIVE ROBERT E. ANDREWS: ONE CAN MAKE a compelling moral case for the proposition that the democratic and freedom-loving people of Taiwan should determine for themselves the shape of their future. It is a moral case that I accept and support, but I'm here this morning to make the case that a policy that recognizes in the first instance the right of self-determination for the people of Taiwan is critical to the strategic interests of the United States of America.

I am a radical democrat with a small *d*. I believe that history teaches us that the security of the American people, the prosperity of the American people, and the welfare of the American people are best served when as many states in as many places as possible practice democracy.

I am hard-pressed to cite any example in modern history—and, in fact, I can think of none—where one democratic state attacked or invaded another democratic state. Democracies don't attack each other because democracies use violence as a last

These remarks were published originally in The Honorable Robert E. Andrews and The Honorable Steve Chabot, "Two Congressmen Look at 'One China,'" Heritage Foundation Lecture No. 821, February 6, 2004 (delivered September 16, 2003), at *www.heritage.org/Research/AsiaandthePacific/hl821.cfm*.

resort, not as a first resort. It is in the best interests of the United States to promote democracy, whether it is in the Middle East, South Africa, Europe, the former Soviet states, or, most especially, in Asia with respect to Taiwan and the People's Republic of China (PRC).

Thirty years from now, whoever is President, whoever is in the Congress of the United States of America, will no doubt face a world in which there is one other dominant country that will vie for influence and power in the economic, diplomatic, and most probably military spheres. That other nation will be the People's Republic of China. The PRC by that time will likely have 1.3 billion people. It will be able to call to arms as many as five times more men and women than the United States can call to arms.

If the economy of the PRC grows for the next 25 years at the pace at which it has grown for the past 25 years, China will enjoy in real terms an economy that is capable of producing a military budget that is almost twice the size of the U.S. military budget today, without spending a greater share of its GDP on the military. The leaders of that nation will not have to choose between guns and butter to produce a military force that will be nearly twice the size of America's military force as it exists today.

Influencing the Future

We have a chance in the next 25 years not to determine that future, but to influence it; to create an environment and create conditions under which the PRC will either evolve toward being a democratic trading partner and ally of the United States or careen toward being a military rival of the United States. The lives our children and grandchildren will live 30 years from now will be darker and more ominous if the second path occurs. In the next two-and-a-half decades, we will have the opportunity to try to influence the evolution of the People's Republic of China toward the first path.

The future of the people of Taiwan is the future of the people of the United States. It's the same issue. The people of Taiwan are confronting that issue today. If we understand what we are doing, we ought to be confronting that issue as well. But whether we understand it or not, over the course of the next two or three decades, we will certainly confront that choice; and that choice is whether we respond in the face of an oligarchic government by compromising our principles or by adhering to them.

The core principle of American democracy in foreign policy should always be the promotion of democracy—not in all ways, not at all times, and not in the same manner in every country, but the core goal and core value should be the propagation of democratic states around the world. Such is the right policy toward the issue of Taiwan in this decade.

There are those who would argue that this would represent a reversal of American policy, most especially since 1979. I would submit that they are wrong in their interpretation of history. More important, they are wrong in their prescription for America's future.

I think that a more studied analysis of the history of our relations in Asia since 1951 would show that the United States has never recognized the idea or the legal claim that the sovereignty of Taiwan is a matter for determination in Beijing. To the contrary, we have always recognized the legal claim that questions about the sovereignty of Taiwan are a matter of negotiation, a matter of mutual assent between the people of Taiwan and their freely and democratically elected government and the government that rules in the People's Republic of China.

Defining "One China"

This seminar, I understand, was organized around the idea of a "one-China" policy. I think we do have a one-China policy. I think we should have a one-China policy. But the definition of that policy should be a matter of mutual assent.

What does that mean? It means to me that if the democratically elected government of Taiwan one day reaches an agreement, which it feels is appropriate for its citizens, that results in Taiwan being part of an integrated China, we should recognize that agreement; however, if such an agreement is not possible, which today it is not, or if it is rejected by the democratic leader-ship of Taiwan, then we should recognize Taiwan as a free and independent state.

There are those who will say that this is unduly provocative, that it will disrupt the relations between the United States and the PRC and lead us toward that dreaded second path of superpower military competition in the next two to three decades. I respect-fully submit that I can't think of an analysis that's more wrong than that, and I believe there's historical precedent for this.

Ronald Reagan and the "Evil Empire"

For years, the policy of the United States toward the Soviet Union after the Second World War was recognition of the inevitability of Soviet rule after Yalta and a policy of mutual coex-istence. Mutually assured destruction was the more ominous artic-ulation of that policy. Détente was the more hopeful articulation of that policy under President Richard Nixon.

In 1981 and 1982, President Ronald Reagan dramatically changed our orientation toward that policy. In a speech to the British House of Commons that was rather mockingly referred to as the "Evil Empire" speech, President Reagan announced a whole new orientation for U.S. policy toward the Soviet Union. Paren-thetically, I must say that those who mock the Evil Empire speech probably have never read it. I would commend it to you.

In this speech, President Reagan said that force is always a last option for the United States and that, in a case of confrontation between nuclear superpowers, force is not even an option at all. But he also said unequivocally that the goal of the United States' policy toward the Soviet Union was the promotion of democracy and human rights within the Soviet Union. This was regarded as a wildly radical proposition in 1982.

One can quarrel about how we got to the events of 1989, 1990, and 1991. There are those who claim that President Reagan's rhetorical leadership was unrelated to those events. There are those who claim that it was pivotal to those events. I'm more of the view that it was pivotal to those events, but the point is that the events occurred. The authoritarian regime within the Soviet Union and its client states collapsed.

There have been many problems since then, but I don't know a Member of Congress or a serious commentator on the world stage who would trade the situation we have today for the one that we had in 1978 when it comes to our relations with what used to be the Soviet Union.

A Policy of Radical Democracy

How did this happen? I believe it happened because the United States practiced a policy of radical democracy when it came to the Soviet Union, and I believe we should practice the same policy when it comes to the People's Republic of China. Our goal with respect to the PRC should be to create conditions under which the PRC can evolve toward a democratic state. It is in our own national interest to do so.

Taiwan is pivotal to that policy. If we are ambiguous about Taiwan's status, then we are ambiguous about Taiwan's moral standing, and we are ambiguous about our own strategic goals. I do not believe we can afford that ambiguity.

Do I advocate military confrontation with the PRC? Of course not. Do I advocate any sort of bellicose policy toward the PRC? Of course not. But I would suggest that any trade decision, any diplomatic decision, any decision that has global scope should be made with the objective of promoting the conditions that would lead to the evolution of a democratic state in that area of the world.

There are two specific signals I think the United States should send with respect to Taiwan and its role in this process.

The first is the vigorous advocacy for Taiwan to be represented in the World Health Organization (WHO). There is a very practical reason for this that did not exist even a year ago: It is called SARS. How much more limited would the effect of SARS have been if Taiwan's government had been fully engaged in the work of the World Health Organization? As a practical matter, it was foolish to maintain that exclusion. As a matter of principle, it was morally bankrupt to maintain that exclusion. I believe the

United States should advocate for Taiwan's inclusion in the WHO and other international bodies.

Second, I think that our half-a-loaf policy toward the sale of defensive weaponry to Taiwan is a mistake. I commend the Bush Administration for its decision—made about 18 months ago—to transfer some radar defensive technology to the Taiwanese. I believe it did not go far enough. I believe that the Aegis radar technology, which is a defensive technology and quite relevant given the military situation in that area of the world, is the appropriate technology that should be transferred to the government of Taiwan.

These will be provocative acts. They represent a very different approach to this problem than we've heard for the past 24 years in this country.

But President Reagan's speech in the House of Commons represented a very different approach to what we had heard about the Soviet Union, and today there is no Soviet Union. There are many problems in that area of the world, but there is much promise and much potential because we stood as radical democrats. That's what we need to do again.

The Choice Before Us

The people of Taiwan stand every day as radical democrats in their lives, in their work, in the conduct of their diplomacy and their governance. I believe we should follow their lead, not simply because it's the right thing to do to support the moral standing of these fine people but because it is in our strategic interest. America is more secure when we are surrounded by democracies.

Given the certainty of the evolution of the People's Republic of China as a major force in world affairs, we have a choice. We can be ambiguous and watch that evolution take place, perhaps toward a bellicose adversary that will recreate the Cold War of the 1950s and 1960s or something worse, or we can create conditions under which that evolution takes place in a very different way toward a democratic, capitalist trading partner of the United States.

The choice that we will face in the next 25 years is the choice that the people of Taiwan face every single day. We should cast our lot with those who practice democracy, with those who don't simply acknowledge American values but who live them. And we should take a lesson from our own values and our own friends and live them in our policy with respect to Taiwan.

REPRESENTATIVE STEVE CHABOT: JUST 10 DAYS AGO, ON September 6 [2003], 150,000 people marched in the streets of Taipei—in the largest demonstration Taipei has ever seen—to demand that government agencies, companies, and private institutions which use "China" in their names replace it with "Taiwan." I don't want to prejudice the issue one way or the other, but I personally see nothing wrong with those sentiments. In fact, I think they are a healthy reminder of what's at stake in Taiwan.

First, let me say that America's interests are my uppermost concern—not just our strategic and economic interests, but, even more important, our interests in protecting and promoting our values as a nation. Those values include democracy, representative government, the rule of law, free markets, and a people's sovereignty over their own nation. These are values that Taiwan's people share with Americans, and it does America no good to avert its eyes when totalitarian states threaten democracies that share our values.

Erosion of American Interests in Taiwan

Over the past several years, I'm afraid I have seen America's interests in Taiwan eroded by a thoughtless reverence for the shibboleth of "one China." Too many Americans—even high government officials—seem to think that one China somehow means that the United States accepts that democratic Taiwan is a part of communist China.

This hit home with me last year, in July of 2002, when I was in China with the House Asia Subcommittee and we had a chance to visit China's National Defense University, which is the major training academy for China's military strategists and thinkers. During our visit, we had pretty frank discussions with Chinese army generals, in which Taiwan came up repeatedly.

The thrust of their position was that Taiwan's separation from China in 1949 was somehow akin to the American Civil War. They pointed to the Chinese civil war, and they tried to justify Beijing's claim to sovereignty over Taiwan and declared China had a right to use force to bring Taiwan under Beijing's control. They were convinced of the legitimacy of the use of force against Taiwan, a legitimacy that was based on their sovereignty over the island. And they thought—because the United States had a one-China policy—that we agreed with their argument.

We explained that Beijing's differences with Taipei should be resolved through diplomacy and through discussions rather than any sort of military action or threat of any type of hostility. I emphasized over and over again that the United States Congress, in particular, had a strong commitment to stand with Taiwan, and I tried to send a clear message to China that—as President Bush has said very clearly—we will "do whatever it takes" to help Taiwan defend itself.

Of course, I said I fervently hoped it wouldn't come to that. Our delegation also hoped that, by making it clear to China that we will stand with Taiwan, that day will never come.

But, in the year since then, China's military buildup continues. If the annual reports our committee gets from the Pentagon are accurate—and I have every confidence that they are—the Chinese People's Liberation Army is amassing an armed force that will be able to launch operations against Taiwan in a matter of years. Already China has deployed a force of 450 short-range ballistic missiles targeted against Taiwan, and that number is increasing at a rate of 75 missiles a year.

Does "One China" Encourage China's War Threats?

Like others, I hope the Chinese military expansion is just intimidation and bluster, but I fear that it is not. And I am coming to a horrifying realization that Washington's one-China policy may actually be encouraging China in its threats of war.

"How?" you ask. Because Chinese leaders think America already agrees that Taiwan is part of China, and they think that America opposes Taiwan's independence.

For the Chinese, that is half the battle. If the United States considers Taiwan as part of China, if the United States opposes Taiwan independence, then the United States must, *ipso facto*, recognize the sovereign right of China to use force to effect the unification of Taiwan with China.

The United States did not, and does not, recognize China's claim to Taiwan. This was clear at the time of our normalization with China in 1979, when we "acknowledged the Chinese position that Taiwan is part of China." But immediately after that, then-Deputy Secretary of State Warren Christopher assured the U.S. Senate, "That is not our position." And in 1982, President Ronald Reagan gave the so-called Six Assurances to Taiwan's president. The Fifth Assurance was that "the United States has not changed its long-standing position on the matter of sovereignty over Taiwan."

And what was that "long-standing" position? As the State Department wrote in a letter to Senator John East in September of 1982, "The United States takes no position on the question of Taiwan's sovereignty." That being the case, it is clear to me—and it should be clear to the Administration—that while America might recognize one China, one China does not include Taiwan.

Taiwan Independence: Fact or Fiction?

It is an incontrovertible fact that the United States treats Taiwan as an independent country. We deal with Taiwan economically, militarily, strategically, politically, diplomatically, commercially, and in every other way as separate from China.

This isn't odd. There is no country on Earth that treats Taiwan as though it were a part of China. Not even China treats Taiwan as if it were part of China—for the obvious reason that there is no People's Republic of China governmental, military, economic, or commercial presence in Taiwan and never has been.

It may be impolite to say so, but "one China" is a fiction—and a dangerous fiction—that most of the international community has bought into in order to mollify China. But ask yourself what sort of a country, much less a major world power, threatens war—even nuclear war—over a fiction?

In February of 2000, when China again threatened Taiwan with armed invasion, President Bill Clinton responded by stating firmly that the United States "will continue to reject the use of force as a means to resolve the Taiwan question. We will also continue to make absolutely clear that the issues between Beijing and Taiwan must be resolved peacefully *and with the assent of the people of Taiwan.*"

It seems to me that if "Taiwan independence" has the assent of the people of Taiwan, then it's not a fiction. And if Taiwan's president says, "Taiwan is an independent, sovereign state, with the 'Republic of China' on this side and the 'People's Republic of China' on that side—one side, one country," that's also no fiction.

I'll tell you what it is: It's an inconvenient truth. Woe betide the political leaders of the United States if they willfully reject the truth simply because it's inconvenient.

When I hear rumors that President George W. Bush is opposed to Taiwan independence, I dismiss them because I know the President doesn't have any philosophical problem with an independent Taiwan. The President and his top foreign policy aides constantly refer to Taiwan as a "country" and sometimes even make the mistake of calling it "the Republic of Taiwan."

This is understandable because Taiwan is not a fiction. Moreover, according to the United States Code—by statute—Taiwan is considered an independent country for the purposes of U.S. law.[1] There is no metaphysical problem anywhere in the U.S. government with an independent Taiwan.

If there *is* opposition to Taiwan independence in the Administration or in the Congress, it is solely because China threatens to go to war with Taiwan if Taiwan declares independence, and

---

[1] Section 4(b)(1) of the Taiwan Relations Act states that "whenever the laws of the United States refer or relate to foreign countries, nations, states, governments, or similar entities, such terms shall include and such laws shall apply with respect to Taiwan."

American leaders know that if there is a war, the United States will help defend Taiwan and that war will be a costly one.

Does "One China" Make War Less Likely?

But does our one-China policy make war less likely? I can't see that it does. In 1938, Britain and France had a virtual "one-Germany" policy which recognized Hitler's claims to the Sudetenland, and Franco–British appeasement on the issue led to Hitler's occupation of Czechoslovakia and ultimately to World War II in Europe.

More recently, in 1990, the U.S. seemed to follow a "one-Arab" policy. On July 25, the American ambassador in Baghdad told Saddam Hussein, "We take no position in territorial disputes between Arabs, like your border disagreement with Kuwait; our only interest is that they be resolved peacefully." As you all know, the "border disagreement with Kuwait" was that Saddam Hussein claimed Kuwait as Iraq's 19th province. The American ambassador's assurance that the United States didn't take any position on the issue only encouraged Saddam to believe that America wouldn't intervene in Iraq's armed invasion of Kuwait.

Why do we have a one-China policy that gives Beijing's leaders the same impression that Saddam had in 1990? The simple answer is that, during the Cold War, the United States saw China as an invaluable ally against the expansion of the Soviet Union, and for two decades, China was a useful partner. China, for its part, set aside its complaints about Taiwan in order to stabilize ties with Washington.

But the Soviet Union is long gone, and with it, the grand organizing principle of the strategic partnership between the U.S. and China has also disappeared. Now the rising hegemonic power in Asia is China. Let's face it: China is a militarily powerful dictatorship. It has an expanding economy, which, by the way, relies on free access to America's markets in order to grow.

So there is no reason, either strategically or economically or morally, why the United States should be timid in the face of China's threats to go to war over Taiwan. China relies on the United States, not the other way around, and as the world's preeminent power, we must not tolerate China's threats.

Would the United States tolerate China's threats of war if Korea did not unify with China? Taiwan is an even bigger market for U.S. exports than South Korea, yet we would never put up with a Chinese demand for suzerainty over Korea. And what about Japan or Southeast Asia? In the 1960s, Chinese revolutionary movements flourished in the region, but we always sided with the independent democracies of Asia against the Chinese dictatorship—except in the case of Taiwan.

Recognizing Reality

With the Cold War over, the Soviet Union extinct, and post-Tiananmen China tightening, not relaxing, its grip on the political, civil, and religious rights of its people, I do not see that humoring China on the Taiwan issue serves America's interests any longer. China is no longer a valued ally against the expansionary, totalitarian Soviet empire. In fact, China itself is a totalitarian state, and by threatening war against a prosperous, dynamic, and militarily potent democracy, China certainly gives the impression of being expansionistic.

Some may ask, "What do you do if China goes to war over Taiwan?" I would answer: "whatever it takes" to defend a democracy against tyranny. I would do it for Korea, for Japan, for the Philippines. It cannot be in America's interests to cede Taiwan, rhetorically or otherwise, to dictatorial China.

Do I want to abandon the one-China policy? I answer that so long as one China is not understood to mean that Taiwan is part of China, then I have no problem with it. But if carelessness or inattention to nuance or force of habit leads America's political leaders to the mistaken conclusion that Taiwan is part of China, then "one China" must be done away with.

The United States must declare that, while we do not support Taiwan independence, neither do we have any philosophical problem with it. If that is what the people of Taiwan want, they have every right to have it. After all, the sovereignty over Taiwan doesn't rest in Beijing or in Taipei, but with Taiwan's people.

8

Understanding and Misunderstanding China Policy: A Primer

JOHN J. TKACIK, JR.

AMERICA HAS HAD A "ONE CHINA" POLICY FOR AS LONG AS I CAN remember—and, being an historian, I have a long memory. But the problem with bumper-sticker diplomacy is that it encourages sloppy thinking, and sloppy thinking in foreign policy leads to dangerous misperceptions.

"One China" does not mean that the United States accepts Beijing's claims to sovereignty over Taiwan. It simply means that the United States recognizes one Chinese government at a time. The State Department understands this and is very careful about phraseology; but the concept is recondite, and the oft-repeated phrase "one China policy" breeds intellectual laziness outside Foggy Bottom.

In May 2002, Deputy Secretary Paul Wolfowitz, speaking off-brief, went so far as to say that the United States's "non-support" of Taiwanese independence was "another of saying we're opposed to" it.[1] Worried telegrams from Taipei flooded the State Department; a few days later, Wolfowitz, responding to virtually the same

---

This paper is an updated version of John J. Tkacik, Jr., "Stating America's Case to China's Hu Jintao: A Primer on U.S.–China–Taiwan Policy," Heritage Foundation Backgrounder No. 1541, April 26, 2002, at *www.heritage.org/Research/AsiaandthePacific/BG1541.cfm*.

question, admitted that he should not have improvised his response. "Sometimes," he explained, "the Russians say that repetition is the mother of learning [and] it's better to say the same thing over and over again than to improvise and I think I even had a lesson a few days ago."[2]

Wolfowitz was obviously suffering from "one China" syndrome, the most visible symptom of which is thinking that "one China" means Taiwan is part of China. It does not, and it is not.

The American view of "one China" is that there is only one legal government of China at a time. It is a guilt-ridden remnant of the 1920s, when paying lip service to China's "territorial integrity" had become an international pastime that permitted no fewer than nine world powers and semi-powers to claim extraterritorial rights in the vast collection of baronies that was China.[3]

On July 25, 1928, driven by a legalistic concern (but not necessarily a practical respect) for the integrity of China's landmass, the United States concluded that Chiang Kai-shek's "Republic of China" (ROC) was about as close as anyone would get to a viable Chinese regime and decided Chiang could represent all China. Through the 1930s, as Tokyo expanded Japan's military occupation of China and established puppet regimes in "Manchukuo," the five northern provinces of Hebei, Chaha'er, Siuyuan, Shanxi, and Shandong, and ultimately a new "central government" in Nanjing under Wang Jingwei in late 1939, Washington resolutely insisted that the sole legal government of China was Chiang's Nationalist government, which had decamped to its wartime capital at Chongqing.

---

[1] U.S. Department of State, "Paul Wolfowitz, Deputy Secretary of Defense, Foreign Press Center Briefing," May 29, 2002, at *http://fpc.state.gov/fpc/10566.htm*. See also Charles Snyder, "Wolfowitz Clarifies Taiwan Stance," *Taipei Times*, May 31, 2002, at *www.taipeitimes.com/news/2002/05/31/story/0000138340*.

[2] See text of Department of Defense, News Transcript, "Deputy Secretary of Defense Paul Wolfowitz Media Availability after IISS Speech," June 1, 2002, at *www.defenselink.mil/transcripts/2002/t06012002_t0601ma.html*.

[3] Those interested in this era of "one China" should read Chapter I, "United States Relations with China with Special Reference to the Period 1944–49," in *A Century of American Policy, 1844–1943*, U.S. Department of State, Publication 3573, Far Eastern Series 30 (Washington: U.S. Government Printing Office, August 1949). Hereafter cited as *China White Paper*.

There is every indication in the record, however, that if Japan had ensured that all those local regimes would grant American businesses the same rights as Japanese businesses, Washington would have been happy to recognize them at some point. For while China's "territorial integrity" (i.e., "one China") was first on the list of the several complaints the United States had lodged with the Japanese imperial government, the key point was the fact that the U.S. "Government reserves all rights of the United States as they exist and does not give assent to any impairment of any of those rights."[4]

Almost by force of habit, Washington continued to view the ROC as the sole legal government of China through World War II and the Chinese civil war. The ROC, however, was defeated by the Communists in 1949 and for all practical purposes (except United Nations representation) was replaced by the "People's Republic of China."

This, of course, is where the "one China" idea broke down. With their defeat in China, the exiled ROC authorities again decamped, this time to the former Japanese colony of Taiwan, where they continued to call themselves the government of China. Rather than having official ties with two Chinas (as the United Kingdom did until 1972), the Americans continued a "one China" policy and in May 1950 prepared to abandon the ROC in Taipei and accept the PRC in Beijing. On May 31, thought was even given to dispatching John Foster Dulles to Taipei, where:

> the Gimo [Chiang] would be approached with word that (a) the fall of Formosa in the present circumstances was inevitable, (b) the US would do nothing to assist Gimo in preventing this, (c) the only course open to the Gimo to prevent the bloodshed of his people was to request UN trusteeship. The US would be prepared to back such a move for trusteeship and would ready the fleet to prevent any

---

[4] *China White Paper*, p. 23.

armed attack on Formosa while the move for trusteeship was pending.[5]

In June 1950, the outbreak of the Korean War made that impossible, and the Americans resigned themselves to continuing the fiction that Chiang Kai-shek was the legal ruler of the mainland. But Washington never acknowledged him as the sovereign ruler of Taiwan.

The corruption of the Chiang regime in mainland China through World War II and the postwar period left Washington with a bad taste in its mouth. Washington was unmoved when Chiang's troops were finally defeated by the Communists.

Moreover, the brutality of Chiang's army of occupation in Taiwan[6] led Secretary of State Dean Acheson to report on April 11, 1947, in a letter to Senator Joseph H. Ball (R–MN), that the transfer of sovereignty over Formosa to China "has not yet been formalized."[7] It is a little-noted fact of diplomatic history that since March 1947, Washington has repeatedly and explicitly *not* recognized ROC sovereignty over Taiwan, and has less repeatedly and not so explicitly refrained from commenting on Beijing's claims to Taiwan—except to "acknowledge" that Beijing has such claims.

Which is why Washington is now in a delicate position vis-à-vis Beijing over Taiwan. In Nixon's landmark "Shanghai Communiqué" of February 1972:

> [The] U.S. side declared: The United States acknowledges that all Chinese on either side of the

---

[5] *Foreign Relations of the United States, 1950, Volume VI, East Asia and the Pacific* (Washington: U.S. Government Printing Office, 1976), p. 348.

[6] The excesses of the occupation were front-page news in Washington within six months of the Nationalist takeover. See "Chinese Exploit Formosa Worse than Japs Did," *Washington Daily News*, March 21, 1946, pp. 1, 3.

[7] U.S. Department of State, Office of the Legal Advisor to the Director of Republic of China Affairs, "Legal Status of Taiwan," July 13, 1971. Reproduced as Appendix C of this volume. The original document is housed at the National Archives and Records Administration, in retired State Department files for the Office of Republic of China Affairs (EAP/ROC) in the POL–19 TAIWAN file. This document was declassified on September 7, 1996.

Taiwan Strait maintain there is but one China and that Taiwan is a part of China. The United States Government does not challenge that position."[8]

Fair enough: As long as both sides claimed to be China, that was their business. But the Chinese side of the Communiqué insisted that China:

> firmly opposes any activities which aim at the creation of "one China, one Taiwan," "one China, two governments," "two Chinas," an "independent Taiwan" or advocate that "the status of Taiwan remains to be determined."[9]

In short, China demanded recognition of its right to impose its will on Taiwan.

In the following decade, the United States issued two more joint communiqués with China, each carefully noncommittal on the matter of Taiwan. In August 1982, President Ronald Reagan approved the last such communiqué, which rhetorically reassured Beijing that the United States "has no intention of infringing on Chinese sovereignty and territorial integrity, or interfering in China's internal affairs, or pursuing a policy of 'two Chinas' or 'one China, one Taiwan.'"[10] Just one month earlier, however, Reagan had communicated to Taiwan's president "six assurances" on the meaning of the upcoming communiqué and averred that "the

---

[8] "Joint Communiqué of the United States of America and the People's Republic of China," issued at Shanghai, People's Republic of China, February 28, 1972. The text of the "Shanghai Communiqué" can be found at the Web site of the U.S. Embassy in Beijing at *www.usembassy-china.org.cn/irc/policy/jtcomm1.html.*

[9] "Joint Communiqué of the United States of America and the People's Republic of China," issued at Beijing, People's Republic of China, January 1, 1979. The text of the "Normalization Communiqué" can be found at the Web site of the U.S. Embassy in Beijing at *www.usembassy-china.org.cn/irc/policy/jtcomm3.html.*

[10] "Joint Communiqué of the United States of America and the People's Republic of China," issued at Beijing, People's Republic of China, August 17, 1982. The text of the "August 17 Communiqué" can be found at the Web site of the U.S. Embassy in Beijing at *www.usembassy-china.org.cn/irc/policy/jtcomm2.html.*

U.S. has not altered its long-standing position regarding sovereignty over Taiwan."[11] Shortly afterward, the Department of State
assured the U.S. Senate that that "[t]he United States takes no
position on the question of Taiwan's sovereignty."[12]

On August 3, 2002, Taiwan's duly elected (and, in March 2004,
re-elected) President Chen Shui-bian had the temerity to say, "Taiwan is our country, and our country cannot be bullied, downgrad-
ed, marginalized, nor treated as a local government." He insisted
that "Taiwan is not a part of any other country, nor is it a local government or province of another country. Taiwan can never be
another Hong Kong or Macau, because Taiwan has always been a
sovereign state."[13] He was simply stating a political fact; but when
he said, "in short, Taiwan and China standing on opposite sides of
the Strait, there is one country on each side," distracted policymakers in Washington had the uneasy feeling that the Taiwan leader
was somehow violating the "one China" policy.

Taiwan is truly the most dynamic and vibrant democracy in
Asia; its human rights record is exemplary; it is one of America's
top 10 export markets. The United States has a security commitment to the island that is embodied in U.S. domestic law as the
Taiwan Relations Act, and U.S. law treats Taiwan as an independent state. But the misuse of the term "one China" has persuaded
policymakers in Washington that somehow we must humor China
into thinking that we accept its claims to Taiwan.

Our China–Taiwan policy is similar to our Israel–Palestine
policy, our policy on the "Turkish Republic of North Cyprus," our

[11] See *China–Taiwan: United States Policy*, Committee on Foreign Affairs, U.S. House of
Representatives, 97th Cong., 2nd Sess., August 18, 1982, p. 33. See also John H.
Holdridge, *Crossing the Divide: An Insider's Account of Normalization of U.S.–China Relations*
(Lanham, Md.: Rowan and Littlefield, 1997), p. 232.

[12] *Taiwan Communique and Separation of Powers*, hearing before the Subcommittee on
Separation of Powers, Committee on the Judiciary, U.S. Senate, 97th Cong., 2nd Sess.,
September 17 and 27, 1982, p. 140.

[13] Republic of China, Office of the President, "President Chen Delivers the Opening
Address of the 29th Annual Meeting of the World Federation of Taiwanese Associations
via Live Video Link," August 3, 2002, at *www.president.gov.tw*. Both Chinese and English
texts are available at the Taiwan Presidential Office Web site by searching Presidential
Statements for August 3, 2002.

"Kashmir" policy, and our erstwhile "East Timor" policy. All are rooted in a recondite diplomacy that produces vague and ambiguous formulae that both sides can insist mean something diametrically opposed to what the other side insists they mean.

This paper accordingly attempts to provide a glossary of the diplomatic arcana surrounding the "one China" debate.

A Glossary of China–Taiwan Policy

The "One China" Policy. Ever since the end of World War II, the United States has evinced a commitment to a "one China" policy that recognizes only one government as the sole legal government of China. In 1949, when Generalissimo Chiang Kai-shek's armies decamped to Taiwan at the end of the Chinese civil war, Washington continued to recognize Chiang's "Republic of China" as the government of all China. In late 1978, Washington announced (in the "Normalization Communiqué," a discussion of which follows) that it would break relations with the regime in Taipei and formally recognize the People's Republic of China (PRC) as the "sole legal government of China."

However, Washington's "one China" policy does not mean that the United States recognizes Beijing's claims to sovereignty over Taiwan.[14] On the contrary, on July 14, 1982, Washington gave specific assurances to Taiwan that the United States did not accept China's claim to sovereignty over the island (a discussion of the "Six Assurances" follows),[15] and the U.S. Department of

---

[14] See, for example, U.S. Department of State, "Transcript: Sec. Powell En Route to Canberra July 29," 2001 (outlining results of visit to Asia Pacific region), at *http://japan.usembassy.gov/e/p/tp-seo259.html.* Powell told reporters that he had raised the issue of the differing American and Chinese views of the "one-China policy": "I think it got us past that, and allowed them to make sure that I had a clear understanding, which I did, of the one-China policy as they see it and allowed me to reinforce to them *our one-China policy understanding* as well, based on the TRA and the three communiqués." Emphasis added.

[15] For a detailed description of the U.S. "one-China" stance, see Ambassador Harvey Feldman, "A Primer on U.S. Policy Toward the 'One-China' Issue: Questions and Answers," Heritage Foundation *Backgrounder* No. 1429, April 12, 2001, at *www.heritage.org/Research/AsiaandthePacific/BG1429.cfm.*

State informed the Senate that "[t]he United States takes no position on the question of Taiwan's sovereignty."[16]

To understand Washington's "one China" policy (to say nothing of Beijing's "one China principle" and Taipei's absolute refusal
to touch "one China" with a ten-foot bamboo stick), it is important
to understand the context of the three separate bilateral communiqués, the plain language of the Taiwan Relations Act of 1979,
the "Six Assurances," "One Country on Each Side," and a host of
other code words that mean different things to different people.

The "Three Communiqués." An often-heard phrase in the
U.S.–China policy lexicon is "the three communiqués."[17] Whenever Beijing is irritated by Washington's contacts with Taipei, the
Chinese allege that the United States has violated its "commitments" in "the three communiqués"—separate bilateral pro-
nouncements made between 1972 and 1982 that establish the
boundaries for U.S. policy toward China.[18] Briefly, these are:

- *The Shanghai Communiqué,* issued by President Richard
  M. Nixon and Chinese premier Zhou Enlai on Febru-
  ary 28, 1972, at the close of Nixon's historic visit to
  China, in which the leaders outlined their respective
  strategic visions;
- *The Normalization Communiqué,* issued by President
  Jimmy Carter and China's Deng Xiaoping on Decem-
  ber 16, 1978, which announced the formal establish-
  ment of diplomatic ties between the two countries; and
- *The August 17 Communiqué,* issued in 1982 by President
  Ronald Reagan and Deng Xiaoping, which stated that

---

[16] *The Taiwan Communiqué and the Separation of Powers,* p. 140.

[17] Internet texts are available at the Web site of the U.S. Embassy in Beijing, at
www.usembassy-china.org.cn/irc/policy/index-c.html.

[18] See James Kelly, Assistant Secretary of State for East Asian and Pacific Affairs, "U.S.
Policy Toward the Asian Pacific Region," Press Briefing, March 14, 2002, at
http://fpc.state.gov/fpc/8787.htm. Kelly stated that "our cross-Strait policy in fact is
unchanged, and it has to do with the familiar language of our one-China policy—bound-
ed by the three U.S.–Sino communiques, governed by the Taiwan Relations Act, and
focused on peaceful resolution across the straits."

the United States "intends to reduce gradually its sales of arms to Taiwan, leading over a period of time to an ultimate resolution" in return for China's adoption of a "fundamental policy" of peaceful reunification with Taiwan.

The Shanghai Communiqué. As a statement of the national strategic visions of China and the United States in the early 1970s, the lengthy Shanghai Communiqué unsurprisingly includes statements of China's support for the North Korean regime and for the Viet Cong, Pathet Lao, and Khmer Rouge revolutions in Indochina. China also stressed its opposition to "the revival and outward expansion of Japanese militarism" and its support for a "neutral Japan" (that is, one not allied with the United States). China's portion asserts that it:

> firmly opposes any activities which aim at the creation of "one China, one Taiwan," "one China, two governments," "two Chinas," an "independent Taiwan" or advocate that "the status of Taiwan remains to be determined."

In the U.S. portion of the communiqué, President Nixon outlined America's interests in Asia. In an effort to convince China that the United States had no preconceptions about the outcome of China's relations with Taiwan, the communiqué states that:

> The United States acknowledges that all Chinese on either side of the Taiwan Strait maintain there is but one China and that Taiwan is a part of China. The United States Government does not challenge that position.

Significantly, however, the United States did not endorse China's position. Furthermore, the U.S. statement does not address the possibility that, at some time in the future, one side of the Taiwan Strait would maintain that it was not part of China.[19] Today, some three decades after the Shanghai Communiqué was signed and after a decade of robust democratic development, Taipei insists that Taiwan is an "independent and sovereign nation" and not a part of the People's Republic of China.[20]

The Normalization Communiqué. In the Normalization Communiqué of December 16, 1978, the U.S. government stated that it "recognizes the Government of the People's Republic of China as the sole legal government of China." The United States subsequently broke relations with the Republic of China on Taiwan, which up to that point it had regarded as the legal government of China. Additionally, "the Government of the United States of America acknowledges the Chinese position that there is but one China and Taiwan is part of China." When questioned on this point during hearings on the Taiwan Relations Act of 1979, the Carter Administration agreed that it had acknowledged the "Chinese position" that Taiwan is part of China but emphasized that *"the United States has not itself agreed to this position."*[21]

However, the Carter Administration conditioned the "normalization" of relations with China on the acknowledgment that the United States would continue to sell military equipment and services to Taiwan. Chinese Communist Party Chairman Hua Guofeng implicitly acknowledged this condition at a press conference on December 16, 1979, when he said that "our two sides

---

[19] The United States clearly knew this was a possibility. In his first meetings with Chinese premier Zhou Enlai in July 1971, National Security Adviser Henry Kissinger cautioned that "if the Taiwan Independence Movement develops without us, that is not in our control." See "Memorandum of Conversation," July 11, 1971, pp. 10–11, at *www.gwu.edu/~nsarchiv/NSAEBB/NSAEBB66/ch-38.pdf.*

[20] President Lee made this assertion several times between 1997 and 2000. See, for example, "President Li Delivers Speech to Paraguayan Parliament," *Taipei Chung-Yang Jih-Pao (Central Daily News),* September 16, 1997, p. 2. See also Ing-wen Tsai, Chairperson of Taiwan's Mainland Affairs Council, "A New Era in Cross-Strait Relations? Taiwan and China in the WTO," Heritage Foundation *Lecture* No. 726, January 14, 2002, at *www.heritage.org/library/lecture/hl726.html.*

[21] Senate Report 96–7, *Taiwan Enabling Act Conference Report, Report of the Committee on Foreign Relations, United States Senate, Together with Additional Views on S. 245,* March 1, 1979, p. 7. Emphasis in original.

had differences on this point" but that China nonetheless agreed to move ahead with normalization.[22]

In fact, the decision to accept continued U.S. arms sales to Taiwan was made by none other than China's "paramount leader," Deng Xiaoping. One U.S. diplomat opined that "Deng Xiaoping's concerns over continuing arms sales to Taiwan were stifled for the moment"[23] by China's strategic imperative of preparing for an imminent invasion of Vietnam (which came on February 19, 1979). Indeed, a senior Chinese diplomat admitted that China "swallowed the bitter pill" of continued arms sales to Taiwan "for strategic reasons."[24]

At no time during the normalization negotiations (conducted directly between Deng and Ambassador Leonard Woodcock) were the Chinese led to believe that the U.S. defense commitment to Taiwan would cease absent the consent of the people of Taiwan. President Carter gave Woodcock explicit instructions on that point.

The August 17 Communiqué on Arms Sales to Taiwan. By 1982, America's robust sales of arms to Taiwan had become politically embarrassing for the Chinese leadership, and Deng Xiaoping ordered his diplomats to re-engage Washington on the issue. Deng wanted a U.S. commitment that it would cease selling weapons to Taiwan, if not at some certain date, then at least at some time in the future.

At that time, the Reagan Administration viewed China as an important strategic Cold War partner against the Soviet Union, especially with respect to the Soviet war in Afghanistan. Though Secretary of State Alexander Haig attempted to persuade President Reagan that China's leaders had "little room to maneuver,"[25] the Administration's negotiators informed the Chinese that the President would not agree to a cessation of arms sales.

In the course of talks leading up to the August 17 Communiqué, the U.S. negotiators acknowledged that the Chinese had

---

[22] *Ibid.*, p. 47. As reported in the U.S. media on December 17, 1979, and a central point in congressional consideration of the Taiwan Relations Act conference.

[23] Holdridge, *Crossing the Divide*, pp. 184–185.

[24] Zhang Wenjin quoted in Holdridge, *Crossing the Divide*, p. 185.

[25] Alexander M. Haig, Jr., *Caveat* (London: Weidenfeld and Nicolson, 1984), p. 214.

stated they "would raise the [Taiwan arms] issue again after normalization."[26] The most the United States would agree to state
was that "it intends to reduce gradually its sales of arms to Taiwan, leading over a period of time to an ultimate resolution."[27]
However, this reduction was conditioned "absolutely" on China's
pursuit of a "peaceful resolution" of its differences with Taiwan.

To avoid any misinterpretations of the diplomatic jargon in
the document, President Reagan issued a presidential letter to
accompany the State Department announcement of the communiqué on August 17, 1982. In that letter, he declared:

> Regarding future U.S. arms sales to Taiwan, our pol-
> icy, set forth clearly in the communiqué, is fully con-
> sistent with the Taiwan Relations Act [of 1979].
> Arms sales will continue in accordance with the Act
> and with the full expectation that the approach of
> the Chinese Government to the resolution of the
> Taiwan issue will continue being peaceful.... The
> position of the United States Government has always
> been clear and consistent in this regard. The Tai-
> wan question is a matter for the Chinese people, on
> both sides of the Taiwan Strait, to resolve. *We will not
> interfere in this matter or prejudice the free choice of, or put
> pressure on, the people of Taiwan in this matter.*[28]

In addition, President Reagan issued a short, confidential presidential directive, initialed by both his new Secretary of State, George
Shultz, and the Secretary of Defense, Caspar Weinberger. It read:

> As you know, I have agreed to the issuance of a joint
> communiqué with the People's Republic of China

---

[26] See Paragraph 2 of the Communiqué.

[27] See Paragraph 5 of the Communiqué.

[28] See Presidential Statement on Issuance of Communique, August 17, 1982, in hearing, *China–Taiwan: United States Policy*, Committee on Foreign Affairs, U.S. House of Representatives, 97th Cong., 2nd Sess., August 18, 1982, p. 33. Emphasis added.

in which we express United States policy toward the matter of continuing arms sales to Taiwan.

The talks leading up to the signing of the communiqué were premised on the clear understanding that any reduction of such arms sales depends upon peace in the Taiwan Strait and the continuity of China's declared "fundamental policy" of seeking a peaceful resolution of the Taiwan issue.

In short, the U.S. willingness to reduce its arms sales to Taiwan *is conditioned absolutely* upon the continued commitment of China to the peaceful solution of the Taiwan–PRC differences. It should be clearly understood that the linkage between these two matters is a *permanent imperative* of U.S. foreign policy.

In addition, it is essential that the quantity and quality of the arms provided Taiwan be conditioned entirely on the threat posed by the PRC. Both in quantitative and qualitative terms, Taiwan's defense capability relative to that of the PRC *will* be maintained.[29]

Further, the President instructed the State Department to inform Congress of the sale of 250 more F5–E fighter aircraft to Taiwan the day after the August 17 Communiqué was issued; on August 18, Assistant Secretary of State John Holdridge so informed the Congress.[30]

The "Six Assurances" to Taiwan. One major complication in the negotiations leading up to the August 17 Communiqué was

---

[29] Emphasis added. For the full text of this short memo, see James R. Lilley and Jeff Lilley, *China Hands: Nine Decades of Adventure, Espionage, and Diplomacy in Asia* (New York: PublicAffairs Books, 2004), p. 248. See also Jim Mann, *About Face: A History of America's Curious Relationship with China, From Nixon to Clinton* (New York: Alfred A. Knopf, 1999), p. 127.

[30] Stephen P. Gibert and William M. Carpenter, eds., *America and Island China: A*

the sudden dismissal of Secretary Alexander M. Haig on June 25, 1982, which Haig attributed in part to his advocacy of the negotiations.[31] With Haig's departure, President Reagan immediately sought to minimize any ill effects the new communiqué might have on morale in Taiwan. On July 14, 1982, a month before the communiqué was to be issued, President Reagan conveyed six White House commitments to Taiwanese President Chiang Ching-kuo. In these "Six Assurances," President Reagan made clear during the course of U.S. negotiations with China that:

1. The United States had not agreed to set a date for ending arms sales to Taiwan;
2. The United States had not agreed to hold prior consultations with the Chinese on arms sales to Taiwan;
3. The United States would not play any mediation role between Taiwan and Beijing;
4. The United States had not agreed to revise the Taiwan Relations Act;
5. The United States had not altered its position regarding sovereignty over Taiwan; and
6. The United States would not exert pressure on Taiwan to enter into negotiations with the Chinese.[32]

These "Six Assurances" have been embraced by all subsequent U.S. Administrations as part of the canon of U.S. policy toward Taiwan.[33] Most recently, on April 21, 2004, Assistant Secretary of

---

Documentary History (Lanham, Md.: University Press of America, 1989), p. 330. See also Patrick Tyler, A Great Wall (New York: PublicAffairs Books, 1999), p. 226. Tyler notes that President Reagan personally informed several Congressmen of the decision on July 28. Former Secretary of State George P. Shultz, in Turmoil and Triumph: My Years as Secretary of State (New York: Charles Scribner's Sons, 1993), pp. 384–385, notes that Holdridge briefed the Senate on the F-5E sale on July 27.

[31] Haig, Caveat, p. 215.

[32] John H. Holdridge, testimony in hearing, China–Taiwan: United States Policy, pp. 15–16. Holdridge described the "Six Assurances" in his memoir, Crossing the Divide, p. 232.

[33] Secretary of State Colin Powell reiterated this during testimony before the Senate

State James Kelly told the House International Relations Committee that:

> Our position continues to be embodied in the so-called "six assurances" offered to Taiwan by President Reagan. We will neither seek to mediate between the P.R.C. and Taiwan, nor will we exert pressure on Taiwan to come to the bargaining table. Of course, the United States is also committed to make available defensive arms and defensive services to Taiwan in order to help Taiwan meet its self-defense needs.[34]

The Sovereignty Issue. Perhaps the most important of the "Six Assurances" has been the fifth—the U.S. position on "sovereignty over Taiwan." This position was explicated in a State Department memorandum to the U.S. Senate in 1970, which said that "as Taiwan and the Pescadores are not covered by any existing international disposition, sovereignty over the area is an unsettled question subject to future international resolution."[35]

Foreign Relations Committee on March 8, 2001. He confirmed that the Assurances "remain the usual and official policy of the United States." See *Hearing of the Senate Foreign Relations Committee for the Fiscal Year 2002 Foreign Operations Budget*, transcribed by Federal News Service, March 8, 2001.

[34] James Kelly, "The Taiwan Relations Act: The Next Twenty-Five Years," testimony before the Committee on International Relations, U.S. House of Representatives, April 21, 2004, p. 40, at http://commdocs.house.gov/committees/intlrel/hfa93229.000/hfa93229_0f.htm.

[35] Cited in Robert L. Starr, "Legal Status of Taiwan," U.S. Department of State, Office of the Legal Advisor (L/EA), Memorandum to Charles Sylvester, Director of the Office of Republic of China Affairs (EA/ROC), July 13, 1971. Reproduced as Appendix C of this volume. The memo is at the National Archives and Records Administration and was declassified on September 7, 1999. See also Tsai, "A New Era in Cross-Strait Relations?" In that lecture, Dr. Tsai, one of Taiwan's most accomplished attorneys, was careful not to assert China's sovereignty over the territory of Taiwan and the Pescadores (Penghu Islands). She acknowledged only that "when the Japanese Government surrendered its sovereignty over Taiwan after the War, the Government of the Republic of China took control and continued to function in Taiwan, after losing the Chinese civil war. However, it gradually lost political recognition from the major countries." This is consistent with the U.S. position that the matter of sovereignty remains undetermined.

The Taiwan Relations Act of 1979. The Taiwan Relations Act,[36] signed by President Carter on April 10, 1979, was designed to ensure that Taiwan would continue to be regarded "as a country for the purposes of U.S. domestic law" despite the lack of formal diplomatic recognition since Washington officially recognized Beijing as the sole legal government of China in 1979.[37]

The first portion of the TRA succinctly outlines the basic elements of U.S. policy toward Taiwan. It declares that Washington's decision to establish diplomatic relations with Beijing depended on China's commitment to resolve its disputes with Taiwan "by peaceful means." The act declares explicitly that is the policy of the U.S. government "to maintain the capacity of the United States to resist any resort to force or other forms of coercion" against Taiwan. Further, the TRA mandates that the United States maintain U.S. defense articles and services "in such a quantity as may be necessary to enable Taiwan to maintain a sufficient self-defense capability."

The "Peaceful Resolution" Cornerstone of U.S.–China Relations. Let there be no mistake: For a quarter-century, the cornerstone of America's strategic relationship with China has been China's commitment to the peaceful resolution of its differences with Taiwan. As the TRA says:

> It is the policy of the United States...to make clear that the United States decision to establish diplomatic relations with the People's Republic of China rests upon the expectation that the future of Taiwan will be determined by peaceful means.

President Reagan instructed his Administration that the "U.S. willingness to reduce its arms sales to Taiwan *is conditioned absolutely* upon the continued commitment of China to the peaceful solution

---

[36] Public Law 96–8; see Appendix B in this volume.
[37] U.S. Senate, *Taiwan Enabling Act Conference Report*, p. 7.

of the Taiwan–PRC differences," a linkage he said "is a *permanent imperative* of U.S. foreign policy."[38]

China's reformist leadership pursued a relatively peaceful approach to Taiwan throughout the 1980s. In the August 17 Communiqué, the Chinese side declared that it had "promulgated a fundamental policy of striving for peaceful unification of the Motherland" and asserted that a "Nine-Point Proposal" of September 1981 was "a further major effort under this fundamental policy to strive for a peaceful solution to the Taiwan question."[39]

In 1986, Beijing began to encourage large numbers of Taiwanese businesses to invest in export-processing operations in China; and in 1987, Taiwan loosened its prohibitions on Taiwan investment in China. As economic and trade relations between China and Taiwan warmed, the overall atmosphere across the Strait improved dramatically. By April 1989, Taiwan's new president, Lee Teng-hui, endorsed the concept of "one China and two equal governments," which would recognize the Communist regime in Beijing as being on an equal status with the government in Taipei.[40] Taipei has insisted since at least 1991 that in any negotiations, Beijing must recognize Taiwan's status as an equal political entity with the People's Republic.[41]

China's leadership, however, was under siege and far too preoccupied with the survival of their regime to respond with any creativity. On June 4, 1989, demonstrations by China's burgeoning pro-democracy movement in Beijing's Tiananmen Square were brutally suppressed by the People's Liberation Army (PLA).

---

[38] Lilley and Lilley, *China Hands*, p. 248. Emphasis added.

[39] The centrality of China's commitment to a peaceful resolution of the Taiwan issue is described by Holdridge in hearing, *China–Taiwan: United States Policy*, pp. 14–15. See also Paul Wolfowitz, "Taiwan Communiqué and Separation of Powers," testimony before the Subcommittee on Separation of Powers, Committee on the Judiciary, U.S. Senate, March 10, 1983, p. 11, and Senate Report No. 98–63, June 1983, p. 4, and footnote.

[40] Daniel Southerland, "Taiwanese Leader Pursues 'Flexible Diplomacy' Toward China," *The Washington Post*, April 15, 1989, p. A15.

[41] Republic of China Executive Yuan (Cabinet), *Guidelines for National Unification*, March 14, 1991. The Executive Yuan asserts that principles of "parity and reciprocity" must govern talks between Taiwan and China.

Beijing's confidence in its own legitimacy vis-à-vis Taipei was further undermined in the 1990s by the fall of communism in Eastern Europe.

China's posture toward Taiwan became increasingly more hostile in the 1990s as the rapidly democratizing Taiwan attempted to assert a separate identity. After the collapse of the Soviet Union, China's military was left without a clear mission and sought to justify its continued modernization by focusing on the mission to "liberate" Taiwan. The PLA modernization effort was structured around a Taiwan invasion scenario and deterrence of U.S. support for the island.

At the core of this activity were efforts to procure advanced arms from the new Russian Federation. In 1992, for example, China made the first purchase on a contract to buy advanced Sukhoi 27 fighter jets. In response, the United States felt compelled to authorize the sale of F–16 fighters to Taiwan.

But the F–16 sale and a French sale of Mirage 2000–5 fighter jets to Taiwan shortly thereafter had a paradoxical effect. Beijing opened a political dialogue with Taipei in October and November 1992. The next year, in April 1993 in Singapore, the personal representatives of Chinese President Jiang Zemin and Taiwanese President Lee Teng-hui met openly for the first time. Apparently seeing Taipei as gaining currency among the Western democracies so shortly after Tiananmen, Beijing felt the need to reengage.

That feeling did not last long. The day after a Taiwan delegation arrived in Beijing in August 1993 to follow up on the progress of the Singapore meetings, Beijing's Foreign Ministry issued a harsh "white paper" on the Taiwan issue, quickly souring relations.[42] On November 21, 1993, Jiang Zemin told a group of reporters at a meeting of the Asia Pacific Economic Cooperation (APEC) forum

---

[42] See *Taiwan Wenti Yu Zhongguode Tongyi* (*The Taiwan Question and the Reunification of China*), State Council Information Office and Taiwan Affairs Office of the State Council of the People's Republic of China, Beijing, August 30, 1993. Known as the "Taiwan White Paper of 1993," the White Paper was translated into English by the U.S. government's Foreign Broadcast Information Service and issued as the FBIS–CHI–93–163 edition of the

in Seattle that "there is only one China, and that is the People's Republic of China, and Taiwan is a province of China."[43]

Responding to Jiang's stance, Taiwan's APEC representative, economic minister P.K. Chiang, asserted to reporters at the Seattle APEC summit that:

> our country and communist China are currently two sovereign states, neither of which is subordinate to the other. Taiwan's policy is for the government to face problems with a practical attitude before the conditions are ripe for reunification (in the hope of) implementing by stages a Two-China policy under the general direction of One China in the Future.[44]

P.K. Chiang explained that "China is a neutral historical, geographical, and cultural name. No doubt Taiwan is part of China, but so is mainland China."[45]

The question of China's commitment to "peaceful resolution" of the sovereignty dispute with Taiwan once again claimed center stage.

China's Missile Buildup Opposite Taiwan

In early 1994, Taiwan's President Lee demonstrated that his country was still highly regarded among its neighbors in Southeast Asia. He visited the Philippines, Indonesia, and Thailand and was feted by heads of state in all three countries in a voyage that the press dubbed "vacation diplomacy."

FBIS "Green Book," pp. 433–453. The original Chinese edition reiterated that the PRC "is the sole legal government of China and Taiwan is a part of China" (p. 7); declared that the United States was responsible for the "Taiwan Question" (p. 9); and stated flatly that Taiwan membership in the United Nations was "out of the question" (p. 25). The Taiwan delegation canceled its talks in Beijing and returned to Taipei on September 2, 1993.

[43] Republic of China Ministry of Foreign Affairs, "Waijiaobu Xinwengao (Foreign Ministry Press Release)," R–T252–1, November 22, 1993.

[44] "Economic Minister Refutes Jiang Zemin's One-China Speech," Taipei China Broadcasting Corporation News Services, Hookup program (in Mandarin), November 21, 1993, transcribed by BBC at 212300 CE/Badgley DB052211.003 MY 22/0751Z NOV.

[45] *Ibid.*

In May 1994, however, Chinese pressure prevented the United States from giving him even token protocol courtesies during a stopover in Honolulu en route to Central America. The snub stung. Mr. Lee made it his top foreign policy priority to get an invitation to the United States, ideally to speak at his doctoral alma mater, Cornell University. A year of patient yet aggressive lobbying yielded the visit in June 1995.

In July 1995, China lashed out in reaction to President Lee's campaign to forge closer ties with the United States. The PLA conducted missile tests in a 32-kilometer–wide area some 85 miles north of Taiwan on the Strait, blocking all maritime traffic into Taiwan's northern ports. The tests included at least six launches of nuclear-capable M–9 missiles. Fearful of angering Beijing, the U.S. Department of State commented only that it believed China's missile tests "do not contribute to peace and stability in the region."[46]

Emboldened by this tepid reaction to the missile tests, China announced a second round of missile tests in the Taiwan Strait on August 10. From August through December 1995, the Chinese continued large-scale military exercises virtually uninterrupted. This was widely seen as a way to intimidate Taiwan's populace before the island's first-ever presidential elections, which were to be held on March 19, 1996.

Veiled Threats Against the United States

By late January 1996, at least one report in *The New York Times* cited Chinese army plans for an attack against Taiwan that would consist of one conventional missile strike a day for 30 days: "Preparations for a missile attack on Taiwan and the target selection to carry it out have been completed and await a final decision by the

---

[46] U.S. Department of State, Daily Press Briefing, July 24, 1995. Spokesman Nicholas Burns told a questioner that "we do not believe this test contributes to peace and stability in the area," adding that "it's been the long-standing policy of the United States to seek to promote peace, security and stability in the area of the Taiwan Strait. This is in the interests of the United States, the People's Republic of China, and Taiwan." Asked whether the United States considers the test a provocation, Burns replied: "We don't believe that it contributed to peace and stability in the area. We've made that clear to the Chinese government."

Politburo in Beijing."[47] A former U.S. diplomat said that Chinese general Xiong Guangkai had asserted that China could act militarily against Taiwan without fear because U.S. leaders "care more about Los Angeles than they do about Taiwan"—apparently an indirect threat to use nuclear weapons against the United States if it were to come to Taiwan's defense.

On March 8, 1996, after several weeks of warnings, China again began missile launches in the area, firing at least four unarmed M–9 medium-range missiles into the sea near Taiwan. Three missiles landed 50 miles from Taiwan off the southern port of Kaohsiung, and one hit within 12 miles of land near the northern port of Keelung, blocking all merchant sea traffic into Taiwan for days. In response to this Chinese aggressiveness, President Clinton ordered two U.S. Navy aircraft-carrier battle groups to the Taiwan Strait area, and there were no further Chinese missile tests in the Strait.[48]

Since 1996, China has maintained this hostile military posture toward Taiwan; and in August 1999, it began sending advanced jet fighters near the Taiwan Strait "center line."[49]

Shortly before Taiwan's second presidential election, slated for March 18, 2000, China issued another "white paper," which called for the use of "all drastic measures possible including the use of force" if Taiwan did not declare itself part of China and agree to negotiations by a date certain.[50] The Chinese threat was

---

[47] Patrick Tyler, "As China Threatens Taiwan, It Makes Sure U.S. Listens," *The New York Times,* January 24, 1996, p. 1. General Xiong is identified as the official in Mann, *About Face,* p. 342.

[48] Art Pine, "U.S. Faces Choice on Sending Ships to Taiwan," *Los Angeles Times,* March 20, 1996, p. A1. See also Steven Mufson, "China Blasts U.S. for Dispatching Warship Groups," *The Washington Post,* March 20, 1996, p. A1.

[49] Zou Jingwen, *Li Denghui Zhizheng Gaobao Shilu (A True Account of Lee Teng-hui's Rule)* (Taipei: Chengyang Publishing, 2001), p. 234.

[50] China State Council, Taiwan Affairs Office and the Information Office, "The One-China Principle and the Taiwan Issue," February 21, 2000, at *http://english.peopledaily. com.cn/features/taiwanpaper/taiwana.html.* The white paper declared, among other things, that the "government of the 'Republic of China'...has long since completely forfeited its right to exercise state sovereignty on behalf of China and, in reality, has always remained only a local authority in Chinese territory," and "if the Taiwan authorities refuse, *sine die,*

so alarming that President Clinton felt compelled to address it
directly in a speech two days later, declaring that:

> we'll continue to reject the use of force as a means
> to resolve the Taiwan question, we'll also contin-
> ue to make absolutely clear that the issues
> between Beijing and Taiwan must be resolved
> peacefully and with the assent of the people of
> Taiwan.[51]

Nonetheless, since then China not only has held continual
military exercises, but also has increased its force of short-range
ballistic missiles (SRBMs) deployed opposite Taiwan. The force
has grown from less than 50 SRBMs in 1999 to between 350 and
400 by April 2002 and to 550 by April 2004, with the inventory
expanding at a rate of 75 missiles a year.[52]

On March 19, 2002, the Director of Central Intelligence
declared that "China continues to upgrade and expand the con-
ventional short-range ballistic missile force it has arrayed against
Taiwan."[53] Commenting on China's ever-growing missile threat to
Taiwan, in a speech in March 2002, Deputy Secretary of Defense
Paul Wolfowitz rhetorically told the Chinese that "building up

---

the peaceful settlement of cross-Straits reunification through negotiations, then the Chinese government will only be forced to adopt all drastic measures possible, including
the use of force, to…fulfill the great cause of reunification."

[51] William J. Clinton, "Remarks by the President to the Business Council," Washington, D.C., February 24, 2000.

[52] Richard P. Lawless, testimony before the Subcommittee on East Asian and Pacific
Affairs, Committee on Foreign Relations, U.S. Senate, April 23, 2004, at *http://foreign.
senate.gov/testimony/2004/LawlessTestimony040422.pdf*. See also Bill Gertz, "China Assembles Missiles Near Coast Facing Taiwan," *The Washington Times*, April 2, 2002, p. A3, and
"Chinese Missiles Concern Pentagon," *The Washington Times*, April 3, 2002, p. A3. Gertz's
news stories were based in part on the National Foreign Intelligence Board's "Foreign Missile Developments and the Ballistic Missile Threat Through 2015: Unclassified Summary of
a National Intelligence Estimate," December 2001, at *www.cia.gov/nic/PDF_GIF_otherprod/
missilethreat2001.pdf*.

[53] George J. Tenet, "Worldwide Threat—Converging Dangers in a Post 9/11 World,"
testimony before the Committee on Armed Services, U.S. Senate, 107th Cong., 2nd
Sess., March 19, 2002.

your missiles" does not appear to be "part of a fundamental policy of peaceful resolution."[54]

During the October 26, 2002, summit meeting in Crawford,
Texas, with President George W. Bush, Chinese President Jiang
Zemin was said to have offered to negotiate with the U.S. on the
reduction or removal of China's missile deployments opposite
Taiwan in return for reduced U.S. arms sales to Taiwan. The U.S.
response was that China should negotiate this with Taiwan, not
with the U.S.[55] Somehow, the Chinese never got the message,
because during July 2004 talks in Beijing with U.S. National Security Adviser Condoleezza Rice, the Chinese complained that they
had never received a U.S. response.[56]

By July 2004, the official Chinese media reported that China's
large-scale military exercises at Dongshan Island were a veiled
warning that the United States should not interfere in the Taiwan Strait:

> Military experts say that the Dongshan Island exer-
> cise held this time by the PLA for the "seizure of
> air control over the Taiwan Straits" is no longer the
> previous "preventive" military drill directed against
> "Taiwan Independence," but rather to a large
> extent, it implies an "active," "initiative," and
> "offensive" military drill, making it one of the tac-
> tics to impose military pressure on Taiwan…. If the

---

[54] Gertz, "China Assembles Missiles Near Coast Facing Taiwan." A Pentagon spokesman
stated on April 2, 2002, that "These missiles are clearly designed to project a threatening posture and to try and intimidate the people and the democratically elected government of Taiwan." See also Gertz, "Chinese Missiles Concern Pentagon."

[55] "ROC, PRC Should Discuss Arms Sales, Missile Issues Between Themselves," Taipei
Central News Agency, December 19, 2002. See also Charles Snyder, "U.S. Likely to
Snub China's Missile Offer," *Taipei Times*, December 20, 2002, p. 1, at *www.taipeitimes.com
/News/front/archives/2002/12/20/187840*.

[56] Yu Huijian, "Zhong Mei Tai Yiti Zai Jiao Jin, Dalu Gaoceng Sici Hui Laisi, Feidan
huan Junshou Mei Bu Huiying" (US–PRC–TW Issues Hots up Again, Four Top-level
Meetings with Rice, US Ignores PRC Missiles-for-Arms Sales Offer), *Taipei China Times*,
July 23, 2004, at *http://news.chinatimes.com/Chinatimes/newslist/newslist-content/
0,3546,110505+112004072300087,00.html*.

exercise in 1996 is targeted at Lee Teng-hui's
proclamation "ROC in Taiwan"; the exercise of
2000 is directed against Chen Shuibian's substan-
tive "Taiwan Independence" policy, the exercise of
2001 is an explicit warning to Taiwan authorities
and the foreign country that attempts to interfere
in the Taiwan Issue not to "play with fire." Then
the exercise this year is a substantial warning to
"Taiwan independence" elements.[57]

It was a message that the Pentagon was finally beginning to
absorb. On May 28, 2004, the annual Pentagon report on the
military power of the PRC observed:

Nevertheless, the PLA's determined focus on
preparing for conflict in the Taiwan Strait—to
include accelerated deployments of short-range
ballistic missiles opposite Taiwan—*casts a cloud over
Beijing's declared policy of seeking "peaceful reunification"* under the "one country, two systems" model.[58]

The U.S. Policy of "Ambiguity"

Within the U.S. State Department, the dissonance between
the reality of the U.S. defense commitment to, and its *de facto*
recognition of, Taiwan and the legal fiction of a "one China" policy has been referred to as "ambiguity." Such ambiguity allows the
United States to pursue normal relations with China so long as it
pretends not to have normal relations with Taiwan.

This "understanding" between Washington and Beijing was
reached in December 1978 and became the subject of a news

---

[57]"PLA to Conduct Maneuvre at Dongshan Is. This Month," *People's Daily* English
Edition, Internet, July 8, 2004, at *http://english.peopledaily.com.cn/200407/08/
eng20040708_148935.html.*

[58]U.S. Department of Defense, *FY04 Report to Congress on PRC Military Power Pursuant to
the FY2000 National Defense Authorization Act: Annual Report on the Military Power of the People's
Republic of China,* May 28, 2004, p. 3, at *www.defenselink.mil/pubs/d20040528PRC.pdf.*
Emphasis added.

commentary by Henry Kissinger on September 7, 1999.[59] In it, Kissinger criticized Taiwanese President Lee for "violating" that "understanding" by declaring the "two states doctrine" on July 9, 1999. What Kissinger failed to acknowledge, however, is that Taiwan has had no part in formulating that "understanding" between China and the United States, and it could hardly be said to be bound by it, especially in light of the "Six Assurances."

"Strategic Ambiguity." The Clinton Administration developed a policy of "strategic ambiguity" about Taiwan after President Lee Teng-hui's private visit to his alma mater, Cornell University, in June 1995. China interpreted the approval of Lee's visa by the U.S. State Department as an indication that the U.S. commitment to "one China" was in danger. Over the following years, the Clinton Administration both cautioned Taipei that it could not necessarily count on U.S. support if China were to take military action against it and told Beijing that it could not rule out the possibility that the United States would intervene on Taiwan's behalf in such a conflict.[60]

This studied indecisiveness was called "strategic ambiguity" by journalists, probably because that was the way their policymaking (but anonymous) sources described it to them. In fact, the term "strategic ambiguity" was coined in October 1995 by Joseph Nye, then Assistant Secretary of Defense for International Security Affairs, who simply said:

> [W]e look at the relationship with China, from a military perspective, it's one of some strategic ambiguity since that we have some common interests with China, we also have some clear differences.[61]

---

[59] Henry Kissinger, "Storm Clouds Gathering," *The Washington Post*, September 7, 1999, p. A19.

[60] Senator Richard Lugar, "Timely Exit for Ambiguity," *The Washington Times*, May 17, 2001, p. A16. See also Michael Dobbs and R. Jeffrey Smith, "U.S. Warships to Reduce China–Taiwan Tensions," *The Washington Post*, March 12, 1996, p. A2.

[61] Joseph Nye, "The Growth and Role of Chinese Military," testimony before the Subcommittee on East Asian and Pacific Affairs, Committee on Foreign Relations, U.S. Senate, October 11, 1995.

The Clinton Administration was aware of the bad press the term inspired, and it was declared, as one former White House aide put it, "anathema in the NSC and [Assistant Secretary of State Winston] Lord went to great lengths to disavow the term in public testimony and speeches."[62]

Still, the "ambiguity" convinced Beijing that the U.S. would, in fact, do nothing if China used military force against Taiwan. Chinese missiles began to fall within 12 miles of the Taiwan coast in March 1996, and President Clinton found it necessary to dispatch two U.S. Navy carrier battle groups to the Strait for Taiwan's defense. It became clear that the policy of "strategic ambiguity" was not sufficient.[63] For the remainder of Clinton's term, however, Washington continued pressuring Taiwan to refrain from "provoking" Beijing.

The Bush Administration has abandoned the "strategic ambiguity" policy.[64]

The Clinton Administration's "Three No's" About Taiwan. The "strategic ambiguity" policy proved confusing. Hardliners in the Chinese leadership saw it as evidence that China's threats against Taiwan (and the United States) were effective. After China launched its first missile "tests" toward Taiwan in July 1995, President Clinton wrote a secret letter to Chinese President Jiang Zemin to articulate, for the first time, the "Three No's" policy of his Administration.[65] That is, the President said, "no two Chinas, no Taiwan

---

[62] Robert L. Suettinger, *Beyond Tiananmen: The Politics of U.S.–China Relations 1989–2000* (Washington, D.C.: Brookings Institution, 2003), p. 259.

[63] See a joint letter by The Heritage Foundation and the Project for the New American Century, August 24, 1999, at *www.newamericancentury.org/Taiwandefensestatement.htm*, calling on the Clinton Administration to "declare unambiguously that it will come to Taiwan's defense in the event of an attack or a blockade against Taiwan." The letter was signed by 25 prominent conservatives, including Richard L. Armitage (now Deputy Secretary of State); John R. Bolton (now Undersecretary of State); I. Lewis Libby (now Vice President Cheney's Chief of Staff); and Paul Wolfowitz (now Deputy Secretary of Defense).

[64] David Lague, "This Is What It Takes," *Far Eastern Economic Review*, April 25, 2002, p. 22. The first sentence reads, "It's unambiguous: 'Strategic ambiguity' is dead."

[65] In *Ta Kung Pao* (Hong Kong), August 3, 1995, quoted in John W. Garver, *Face Off: China, the United States and Taiwan's Democratization* (Seattle: University of Washington Press, 1997), translated by Foreign Broadcast Information Service (FBIS).

independence, no Taiwan membership in the United Nations."[66] The Chinese press characterized President Clinton's position in the letter as "opposing" Taiwan's separate status from China.

Although President Clinton's letter was publicized in both the Chinese and Taiwan press, it was not printed in the U.S. media. By the time Jiang Zemin made a state visit to the United States in October 1997, the substance of the letter had been assimilated into the State Department lexicon. It was uttered a few times during that visit and later became a State Department formulation for China policy.[67]

After that, the Clinton Administration insisted that it did not "support" Taiwan's separate identity, but it also never stated that it "opposed" it.[68] China made the "Three No's" a touchstone of U.S.–China relations and insisted that President Clinton publicly declare them on his state visit to China in June 1998. The President obliged.[69]

---

[66] These principles were first raised in 1971 by Zhou Enlai in his secret meetings with Kissinger. At the time, Kissinger said that "we did not advocate a 'two Chinas' or a 'one China, one Taiwan' solution, but would accept any political evolution agreed to by the parties, we hoped that this evolution would be peaceful, and Chou said the PRC would try to keep it so." However, Kissinger also stressed that "some events in Taiwan might be beyond our ability to control." See Henry Kissinger, "Memorandum to the President," July 14, 1971, p. 13. An image file of the memorandum is available at the National Security Archive Web site at *www.gwu.edu/~nsarchiv/NSAEBB/NSAEBB66/ch-40.pdf*.

[67] State Department spokesman Jamie Rubin explained, "We certainly made clear that we have a one China policy, that we don't support a one China or one Taiwan policy, we don't support a two China policy. We don't support Taiwan independence, and we don't support Taiwanese membership in organizations that require you to be a member state. We certainly made that very clear to the Chinese." See U.S. Department of State, Daily Press Briefing, October 31, 1997, at *http://secretary.state.gov/www/briefings/9710/971031db.html*.

[68] The State Department apparently does not construe "no support" as meaning "oppose." In a different context, State Department spokesman James Foley was asked, "Do you all oppose independence for Kosovo under any circumstances at any time?" Foley replied, "well, we have made clear that we do not support Kosovo independence. I don't care to elaborate on that." See U.S. Department of State, Daily Press Briefing , February 11, 1999, at *http://secretary.state.gov/www/briefings/9902/990211db.html*.

[69] "I had a chance to reiterate our Taiwan policy, which is that we don't support independence for Taiwan, or two Chinas, or one Taiwan–one China. And we don't believe that Taiwan should be a member in any organization for which statehood is a requirement. So I think we have a consistent policy." See Office of the White House Press Secretary, "President's Comments at the Shanghai Library," June 30, 1998.

As explained more fully below, the Bush Administration does not support the "Three No's" policy toward Taiwan.[70]

Taiwan's "Two States" Doctrine. Taiwanese President Lee Teng-hui and many other Taiwanese were stunned by President Clinton's "Three No's" public statement in China in 1998. Lee ordered a comprehensive reappraisal of Taiwan's stance on China, which took a year to complete. On July 9, 1999, he articulated what could be called a "two China" doctrine in an interview with *Deutsche Welle.* According to Lee:

> since our [Taiwan's] constitutional reform in 1991, we have designated cross-strait ties as nation-to-nation, or at least as special state-to-state ties, rather than internal ties within "one China" between a legitimate government and a rebellion group, or between central and local governments.[71]

Taiwan's new government under Chen Shui-bian has refrained from using the term "state-to-state ties" to describe Taiwan's posture toward China. Its stance on Taiwan's sovereignty is that "the Republic of China has been a sovereign and independent nation since 1912" and that both Beijing and Taipei should continue:

> to debate, among themselves and in the international setting, on the sovereignty issues. Despite the sovereignty controversy, it is very clear that each side exercises full control and jurisdiction over a

---

[70] Spokesman Richard Boucher confirmed the demise of the formulation: "If I were to go back into the entire history of the Three No policy, you would find it wasn't ever stated quite the same way, and I don't intend to state it that way today. We adhere to the One China policy, and I will stick with that. And if we decide to say more, I will get back to you." See U.S. Department of State, Noon Briefing, March 19, 2001, at *www.state.gov/r/pa/prs/dpb/2001/1420.htm.*

[71] "VOG [Voice of Germany] Interviews Li Teng-hui," Taipei *Chung-Yang Jih-Pao (Central Daily News)*, Internet version, in Chinese, July 10, 1999, translated by Foreign Broadcast Information Service as document FTS19990712000518.

clearly delineated territory and there is no issue of political subordination to each other. The Republic of China on Taiwan does exist, and is a full-functioned country.[72]

President Chen Shui-bian has, however, lent his prestige to the use of the term "state-to-state." Despite its non-use in public, the "state-to-state" formulation remains at the core of Taiwan's policy approaches toward China.[73] Chen added his own formulation to the glossary of "one China": *Yibian Yiguo* (one country on each side). On August 3, 2002, he announced this new approach:

> Taiwan is our country, and our country cannot be bullied, downgraded, marginalized, nor treated as a local government. Taiwan is not a part of any other country, nor is it a local government or province of another country. Taiwan can never be another Hong Kong or Macau, because Taiwan has always been a sovereign state. In short, Taiwan and China standing on opposite sides of the Strait, *there is one country on each side.* This should be clear.[74]

Chen held tightly to the "one country on each side" of the Taiwan Strait formula for the next 20 months and through his reelection campaign in early 2004. He repeated it several times

---

[72] Tsai, "A New Era in Cross-Strait Relations?"

[73] Former President Lee Teng-hui shared the stage with President Chen Shui-bian at an "Academia Historica" seminar on Taiwan history. He declared that "special state-to-state" relations had become the "bottom line" in cross-strait negotiations. See "'State-to-State' the Bottom Line: Lee," *Taipei Times*, October 24, 2001, at *www.taipeitimes.com/news/2001/10/24/story/0000108454*. President Chen's top China policymaker, Dr. Tsai Ing-wen, is said to have been the architect of the "Special State-to-State" formulation in 1999. See also Zou Jingwen, *Li Denghui Zhizheng Gaobao Shilu (A True Account of Lee Teng-hui's Rule)*, pp. 222–226.

[74] Republic of China, Office of the President, "President Chen Delivers the Opening Address of the 29th Annual Meeting of the World Federation of Taiwanese Associations via Live Video Link," August 3, 2002, at *www.president.gov.tw*. Emphasis added. Both Chinese and English texts are available at the Taiwan Presidential Office Web site.

himself during the period.[75] At one point, his top political ally had to refute claims that the president had promised the United States he would not raise the subject.[76] By September 2003, even his pro-China political opposition began to adopt the phrase in hopes of bolstering their support among the electorate in rural Taiwan.[77]

However, in April 2004, after Chen had won reelection to another four-year term, his new foreign minister, Mark Tangshan Chen, admitted that the international pressure was becoming unbearable. While the phrase "describes the status quo," Minister Chen said, "our foreign friends misunderstand it." On the other hand, he added, saying that "Taiwan is a sovereign and independent nation" is perfectly acceptable. The ROC has always been sovereign and independent, he said: "the ROC is on Taiwan, and this is something everyone in the country can accept."[78]

The Bush Policy: Unequivocal Support for Taiwan

Prior to the *Yibian Yiguo* controversy, President George W. Bush's support for Taiwan was firm. In an interview with ABC News on April 25, 2001, President Bush was asked, "if Taiwan were attacked by China, do we have an obligation to defend the Taiwanese?" He responded, "Yes, we do...and the Chinese must

---

[75] For example, see Lin Zhenbo Chen Jiabong, "Bian: *Yibian Yiguo*, Gongtou Jiu Shi Danghun" ("Chen Shui-bian: One Nation Each Side Is Soul of the Party"), *Taipei China Times*, Internet Edition, August 13, 2003, at *http://news.chinatimes.com/Chinatimes/ newslist/newslist-content/0,3546,110502+112003081300018,00.html.*

[76] "Bu Ti Yibian Yiguo? Wo Bing Wei Xiang Mei Baozheng!" ("Won't Raise One Country on Each Side? We Never Promised that to the Americans!"), *Taipei China Times*, August 13, 2003, at *http://news.chinatimes.com/Chinatimes/newslist/newslist-content/ 0,3546,110502+112003081300020,00.html.*

[77] "Yibian Yiguo, Song: Yibian Qiongren Yibian Caituan" ("One Side, One Country, Song" One Side Is Poor People, One Side Is Wealthy"), *Taipei United Daily News,* July 27, 2003, citing a Central News Agency report of July 26, 2003.

[78] Xu Xiaoci, "Chen Tangshan: Yibian Yiguo Lunshu Ke Tiaozheng" ("Mark Chen Says One Country on Either Side Formula Can Be Adjusted"), *Taipei China Times,* April 30, 2004, at *http://news.chinatimes.com/Chinatimes/newslist/newslist-content/ 0,3546,110502+112004043000038,00.html.*

understand that," adding that the United States would do "whatever it takes to help Taiwan defend herself."[79]

The same day—his 100th day in office—President Bush reiterated the U.S. obligation to "help Taiwan defend herself" under the Taiwan Relations Act in interviews with other major U.S. news media, such as CBS, NBC, CNN, and *The Washington Post*. He said, for example:

> The Chinese must understand that we've got common interests; but there's going to be some areas where we disagree and, evidently, one area where we disagree is whether or not the United States ought to provide defensive arms for Taiwan, which I have done.[80]

In his CNN interview, Mr. Bush also said, "I certainly hope Taiwan adheres to the 'one China' policy, and a declaration of independence is not the 'one China' policy."[81] Nonetheless, his

---

[79] See transcript of President Bush's remarks on *Good Morning, America*, April 25, 2001, at *http://abcnews.go.com/sections/GMA/GoodMorningAmerica/GMA010425Bush_100days.html*. All of these appearances occurred on April 25, 2001. On the CBS *Early Show*, President Bush acknowledged that Beijing and Washington disagree on "the extent to which the United States upholds its obligations under the Taiwan Relations law and…I've upheld our obligations in a very serious fashion, providing equipment for Taiwan so she can defend herself." On the NBC *Today Show*, he averred that "I'm going to fully implement, I'm going to abide by the spirit of the Taiwan Relations law" and pledged to make decisions "that will help Taiwan defend herself and we will help Taiwan defend herself, that the spirit of the Taiwan Relations law and I will continue over my time as president to review Taiwan's defensive needs and if I think it's in our country's interest to sell [weapons] to them." In his CNN interview, Bush said that "my administration strongly supports the 'one China' policy, that we expect that any dispute to be resolved peacefully…. [N]othing has really changed in policy as far as I'm concerned."

[80] The Taiwan Relations Act (22 USC 3301) mandates that the United States be able to resist Chinese force against Taiwan and provide Taiwan with sufficient arms for its self-defense. TRA Section 2(b)(6) states: "It is the policy of the United States—to maintain the capacity of the United States to resist any resort to force or other forms of coercion that would jeopardize the security, or the social or economic system, of the people on Taiwan." Section 3(a) mandates that the United States "will make available to Taiwan such defense articles and defense services in such quantity as may be necessary to enable Taiwan to maintain a sufficient self-defense capability."

[81] "President Bush Says U.S. 'Will Do What It Takes' to Defend Taiwan," transcript of

"whatever it takes" statement was viewed in some quarters with alarm despite the fact that it clearly conforms with the policies of five successive U.S. Administrations and is in fact mandated by the Taiwan Relations Act.[82]

President Bush has put his declaration to "do whatever it takes" to help Taiwan defend itself into action by improving military cooperation with Taiwan, supporting dignified receptions for Taiwanese leaders who visit the United States, and offering repeated support for Taiwan even during two visits to China—something no other U.S. President was prepared to do. As one scholar describes it, President Bush, during his China trips in October 2001 and February 2002, "showed a willingness to meet Chinese leaders' symbolic needs for summitry, while sustaining a tough U.S. stance on bilateral differences and limiting U.S. requests for Chinese support."[83]

In April 2001, President Bush approved the largest single tranche of defense equipment to Taiwan, including four Kidd-class destroyers, eight diesel submarines designed to counter blockades and invasions, 12 P–3C Orion Aircraft, and Paladin self-propelled artillery systems valued at over $4 billion.[84] Moreover, sometime in 2004 or early 2005, the White House will review Taiwan's request for Aegis destroyers, which are able to perform search and missile-guidance functions and can track 100 or more targets simultaneously—a package that could easily top $4 billion all by itself.

Regarding China, Administration officials now refer to the U.S.–China relationship as "candid, constructive, and cooperative."

CNN *Wolf Blitzer Reports*, April 25, 2001, at *http://cnnstudentnews.cnn.com/TRANSCRIPTS/0104/25/wbr.00.html.*

[82] "Whatever it takes" is now a part of official U.S. policy. On March 11, 2001, Deputy Secretary of Defense Paul Wolfowitz said in a closed-door speech that "as President [George W.] Bush and others have said, the United States is committed to doing whatever it takes to help Taiwan defend itself." See Andrea Shalal-Esa, "U.S. Vows to Do What It Takes to Aid Taiwan Defense," Reuters, April 9, 2002. The full text of the speech was made available to Reuters and Bloomberg news agencies under a Freedom of Information Act request.

[83] Robert Sutter, "Grading Bush's China Policy: A–," Center for Strategic and International Studies, March 8, 2002, at *www.csis.org/pacfor/paco210.htm.*

[84] At the time, the value was estimated to be $4 billion. However, the cost of the submarine package alone is now considered to be over $10 billion.

Secretary of State Colin Powell used this description in testimony before the House Committee on International Relations in February 2002:

> A candid, constructive, and cooperative relationship is what we are building with China—candid where we disagree, constructive where we can see some daylight, and cooperative where we have common regional or global interests.[85]

But the Taiwanese president's August 2002 declaration of two countries facing each other on each side of the Taiwan Strait alarmed the Bush Administration just as it was powering up its international campaign to disarm Iraq. In August 2002, Deputy Secretary of State Richard Armitage flew to Beijing, probing for China's position on Iraq. In an August 26 news conference in Beijing, Armitage told reporters that while Taiwan is "one of the questions" about which Washington and Beijing "have a difference of opinion," the U.S. policy on Taiwan "is based on our One-China Policy, the Three Communiqués, and the Taiwan Relations Act."[86]

"Oppose" Taiwan Independence Versus "Not Support." Armitage reiterated that the U.S. "did not support Taiwan independence," but when asked why he used that wording rather than "oppose Taiwan independence," he replied:

> The wording is important. By saying we do not support, it's one thing. It's different from saying we oppose it. If people on both sides of the Strait came to an agreeable solution, then the United States obviously wouldn't inject ourselves. Hence, we use

[85] Colin L. Powell, testimony at budget hearing before the Committee on Foreign Relations, U.S. Senate, February 5, 2002, at *www.state.gov/secretary/rm/2002/7797.htm*.

[86] U.S. Department of State, International Information Programs, "Transcript: Armitage Says US Does Not Support Taiwan Independence (Armitage also discusses South Asia, nonproliferation, terrorism)," August 26, 2002, at *http://usinfo.state.gov/regional/ea/uschina/armit826.htm*.

the term we don't "support" it. But it's something
to be resolved by the people on both sides of the
question.[87]

Yet, two months later, during his October 2002 summit with
Chinese President Jiang, President Bush apparently said he was
"against Taiwan independence." When asked about rumors to
this effect, Assistant Secretary of State James Kelly told reporters
that the important thing is that "the United States does not support Taiwan independence, there is no change in this policy," and
added that observers "need not place too much emphasis on the
exact words that were used."[88]

For some reason, President Bush seemed to favor the idea of
saying he was "against Taiwan independence" despite the urging of
the State Department that he adhere to the "not support" formula.
A year later, during President Bush's October 19, 2003, meeting
with new Chinese President Hu Jintao at the APEC Summit in
Bangkok, Thailand, President Bush apparently repeated his "opposition" to Taiwan independence. President Hu made a point of
telling the press that "President Bush restated his government's
position of adhering to the one China policy, the three China–U.S.
joint communiqués, *and his opposition to Taiwan independence.*"[89]

A White House official, presumed to be National Security
Adviser Condoleezza Rice, briefed reporters later on background
that President Bush had indeed made his "opposition" to Taiwan
independence known to President Hu. When Taiwan journalists
in Washington pressed another unnamed U.S. official about
Bush's exact words and asked whether Bush was misquoted by Hu
as "opposing" independence, the U.S. official said, "I'm not going

---

[87] *Ibid.*

[88] Liu Ping, "Kelaofu Fenghuishang, Buxi Miangao Jiang Zemin: Mei Fandui Taidu" ("At
Crawford Summit, Bush Personally Told Jiang Zemin: United States Opposes Taiwan Independence"), *Taipei China Times,* November 21, 2002, at *http://news.chinatimes.com/Chinatimes/
newslist/newslist-content/0,3546,110505+112002112100067,00.html.*

[89] U.S Department of State, "Remarks by President Bush and President Hu Jintao of
China at the Grand Hyatt Erawan Bangkok, Bangkok, Thailand," October 19, 2003, at
http://fpc.state.gov/fpc/25363.htm. Emphasis added.

to get into a semantic game here—does he not support, does he oppose, is it only moves toward independence."[90]

On November 13, 2003, the chairman of the American Institute in Taiwan, Therese Shaheen, told a Voice of America interviewer that she had been briefed by participants in the Bush–Hu meeting in Bangkok and had been told that Bush had not said the U.S. opposed Taiwan independence:

> Of course I wasn't there. But it was briefed to me. It was briefed to me by people whom I believe, by authoritative sources. And those sources say that that is not correct, that President Bush said we do not support Taiwan independence, which has been our long-standing position. And of course, as you know, as Deputy Secretary Armitage has explained, do not support means we will not take any active role or position in the dispute.... It's really important to know and it's sometimes confusing when we use the words "do not support independence," sometimes people can turn that around because normally in English language you could flip it and it would have the same meaning. And in the case of the United States, it doesn't have the same meaning. It means we are not going to be active in the outcome. We are active in the process. Peaceful, peaceful, peaceful, and that's our mantra, peaceful resolution, and that includes the agreement of people on both sides of the straits.[91]

The Chinese government lashed out immediately. The difference between "do not support" and "oppose" was quite important

---

[90] Charles Snyder, "U.S. Officials Rush to Clear Up 'Independence' Clouds," *Taipei Times,* October 22, 2003, p. 3, at *www.taipeitimes.com/News/taiwan/archives/2003/10/22/2003072879.*

[91] Edited transcript of VOA interview with Therese Shaheen, Chair, American Institute in Taiwan, provided to the author by the interviewer.

to them, and they insisted that President Bush indeed "opposes" Taiwan independence. Foreign Ministry spokesman Liu Jianchao denounced Shaheen's explication of the oppose/not-support debate and insisted vehemently that "U.S. leaders reiterated before Chinese leaders on many occasions that the United States...opposed Taiwan independence." Liu considered it

> ridiculous for Ms. Shaheen to behave that way....
> [I]t's better for people like Shaheen to be well
> aware of the sensitiveness of the Taiwan issue and
> the danger of Taiwan separatists, and behave dis-
> creetly to avoid being completely ensnared by the
> Taiwan separatists.[92]

Shaheen's comments made the Chinese leadership all the more determined to get President Bush on the record as "opposing" Taiwan independence. Over the Thanksgiving weekend, President Bush dispatched his National Security Council Asia staff director, James Moriarty, to Taipei with a personal letter of introduction and a personal verbal message to his Taiwan counterpart. By this time, even the State Department feared that Bush would formalize his "opposition" to Taiwan independence. As one source reported:

> [F]eedback today confirms...that State, including
> Secretary Powell, is very, very unhappy with how
> the NSC handled the Moriarty visit.... [N]o one
> wants to admit this...but it turns out that Powell
> felt constrained to send Bush a letter reminding
> him of the acceptable ways to discuss what the U.S.
> "opposes", and why any changes in the mantra can

---

[92] "Waijiaobu Bosu suowei 'Meiguo Zai tai Xiehui' Fuzeren she Tai Yanlun" (Foreign Ministry Refutes the Argumentation Involving Taiwan from the Responsible Person at the So-Called 'American Institute in Taiwan'"), *People's Daily*, Internet Edition, November 16, 2003, at *www.peopledaily.com.cn/GB/shizheng/1027/2191546.html*. The text of the Foreign Ministry spokesman's statement is available at *www.fmprc.gov.cn/chn/xwfw/fyrth/t42316.htm*.

themselves be de-stabilizing. Sources familiar with the Bush/Hu letter confirm our Report last night, that it did use the "approved" or "time tested" language that the U.S. "opposes" unilateral moves by either China or Taiwan which might upset the peaceful *status quo*.[93]

Secretary Powell's letter did the trick. The White House backed away from expressing to Taiwan its "opposition" to Taiwan independence. But the message was implied, and it did not deter the visiting Chinese premier Wen Jiabao from asking President Bush once again to express his "opposition to Taiwan Independence"— at least in private. When Premier Wen was asked about his meetings with Bush on December 9, he cheerfully replied:

On many occasions, and just now in the meeting, as well, President Bush has reiterated the U.S. commitment to the three Sino–U.S. Joint Communiqués, the one-China principle, *and opposition to Taiwan independence.* We appreciate that. In particular, we very much appreciate the position adopted by President Bush toward the latest moves and developments in Taiwan—that is, the attempt to resort to referendum of various kinds as excuse to pursue Taiwan independence. We appreciate the position of the U.S. government.[94]

President Bush did not contradict his guest, and State Department officials subsequently confirmed—in private—that it was indeed the third time the President had told the Chinese he was "against Taiwan independence." Beijing was ecstatic.

---

[93] Chris Nelson, "STEEL…as Expected, EU Happy China–Taiwan…State Is Worried NSC Maybe Tilting Too Far," *The Nelson Report*, December 4, 2003. Punctuation as in original.

[94] White House, Office of the Press Secretary, "Remarks by President Bush and Premier Wen Jiabao in Photo Opportunity," December 9, 2003, at *www.whitehouse.gov/news/releases/2003/12/20031209–2.html*. Emphasis added.

China's Foreign Ministry, calling Taiwan "the most important and sensitive [issue] in U.S.–China relations," hailed the continuing improvement in Sino–U.S. relations following the Wen visit, which Beijing called "a complete success." "We appreciate President Bush's statement," said Foreign Ministry spokesman Liu Jianchao.[95] President Hu Jintao followed up with a personal phone call to President Bush on December 21 and warned that Taiwan's leader was undeterred in his push for independence.[96] As recently as August 2004, Chinese scholars continued to insist that, "when meeting Chinese leaders, Bush has on many occasions used the expression 'opposed to Taiwan independence'" while nevertheless adding parenthetically, "but the expression 'no support for Taiwan independence' is still used in official US statements."[97]

A garbled message from Washington, however, was all that seemed to reach Beijing. According to CNN's noted China-watcher Willy Wo-lap Lam, Beijing was convinced that Washington's abandonment of its long-standing support for Taiwan carried "much more than semantic or symbolic significance." Lam reported that a "party source" had quoted a "Politburo member" as saying, "If Chen Shui-bian were to disturb the status quo via holding referendums and other means, and we were to respond militarily, the U.S. can't raise objections let alone interfere." The Politburo member added, "we've finally got the Americans right where we want them."[98]

Where "One China" Stands as U.S. Policy

In 2004, as China escalated not only its military expansion program, but also its hostile rhetoric against Taiwan and other

[95] John Pomfret, "Beijing Applauds U.S. Stance on Taiwan: Rare 'Thank You' Follows Bush's Opposition to Moves Toward Independence," *The Washington Post*, December 11, 2003, at *www.washingtonpost.com/wp-dyn/articles/A56250–2003Dec11.html.*

[96] Philip P. Pan, "China Thanks Bush for Taiwan Stance—Beijing Issues New Warning Against Move Toward Independence," *The Washington Post*, December 22, 2003, p. A22.

[97] Wang Jisi, "Meiguo Zhanlue Tiaozheng Dui Zhong Mei Guanxide Yingxiang" ("Impact of US Strategic Adjustment on Sino–US Relations"), Beijing *Xuexi Shibao* (*Study Times*), Internet version, August 16, 2004, at *www.china.org.cn/chinese/zhuanti/xxsb/636512.htm.*

[98] Willy Wo-Lap Lam, "China Claims a Big Win over Taiwan," CNN.COM, December 15, 2003, at *http://edition.cnn.com/2003/WORLD/asiapcf/east/12/15/willy.column/index.html.*

Asian nations (particularly Japan), American policy statements about "one China" have become more guarded.

On April 21, 2004, Assistant Secretary Kelly testified before the House Committee on International Relations and presented the "core principles" of the U.S. government's policy on China and Taiwan:

- The United States remains committed to a China policy based on the three Joint Communiqués *and the Taiwan Relations Act*;
- The U.S. does not support independence for Taiwan or unilateral moves that would change *the status quo as we define it*;
- For Beijing, this means no use of force or threat to use force against Taiwan. For Taipei, it means exercising prudence in managing all aspects of cross-Strait relations. For both sides, it means no statements or actions that would unilaterally alter Taiwan's status;
- The U.S. will continue the sale of appropriate defensive military equipment to Taiwan in accordance with the Taiwan Relations Act; and
- Viewing any use of force against Taiwan with grave concern, we will maintain the capacity of the United States to resist any resort to force or other forms of coercion against Taiwan.[99]

Kelly also told the committee that "it is now undeniable that Taiwan identity has emerged as a political and social issue on the island that figures in election campaigns." He fully appreciated that Taiwan's new identity creates a momentum toward formal independence, which, he said, "will avail Taiwan of nothing it does not already enjoy in terms of democratic freedom, autonomy, prosperity and security." He warned that the PRC could react with "a dangerous, objectionable and foolish response...that

---

[99] Kelly, "The Taiwan Relations Act: The Next Twenty-Five Years," p. 14. Emphasis added.

could destroy much of what Taiwan has built" and "would damage China, too."[100]

Clearly, the message to both sides is that the United States is prepared to be involved in a Taiwan Strait War, whatever the provocation, but that both Taiwan and China must consider the devastating consequences. The answer, Kelly said, was that the People's Republic should "renounce the use of force regarding Taiwan" and that the United States had made "consistent representations stating they should do so." Failing that, Kelly urged both sides "to pursue dialogue as soon as possible through any available channels, without preconditions."[101] He later added that an "appropriate accommodation" should be "worked out by those sides on an equal basis."[102]

This, of course, is anathema in Beijing. As noted above, China's precondition is that Taipei admit that it belongs to "one China" and furthermore that Taipei is subordinate to Beijing. Taiwan's president still pleads for talks "without preconditions" and "on an equal basis," and in this he has American support. Washington's idea of "one China" is beginning to look more like Taipei's than Beijing's.

Indeed, Secretary Kelly admitted at the April 21 hearings that when it came to "our one China, I did not really define it. I'm not sure I very easily could define it."[103] However:

> I can tell you what it is not. *It is not the One-China policy or the One-China principle that Beijing suggests,* and it may not be the definition that some would have in Taiwan. But it does convey a meaning of solidarity of a kind among the people on both sides of the Strait that has been our policy for a very long time.[104]

---

[100] *Ibid.*, p. 15.
[101] *Ibid.*, p. 14.
[102] *Ibid.*, p. 37.
[103] *Ibid.*, p. 32.
[104] *Ibid.* Emphasis added.

When one considers that the U.S. "one China" policy is based on the "Three Communiqués" (which are all agnostic on the matter of "one China") and the Taiwan Relations Act (which regards Taiwan as a country for the purposes of U.S. domestic law[105]), the phrase "one China" appears to have lost any meaning. In fact, Secretary Kelly asserts that he "made the point of [calling it] our one China" policy in an effort to distance it from Beijing's policy."[106]

U.S. Support for Democratic Taiwan

Perhaps Secretary Powell has articulated U.S. policy toward Taiwan most eloquently. "People tend to refer to Taiwan as 'The Taiwan Problem,'" he complained, adding that "I call Taiwan not a problem, but a success story. Taiwan has become a resilient economy, a vibrant democracy and a generous contributor to the international community."[107]

At the April 21, 2004, House hearing, Assistant Secretary of Defense Peter Rodman pointed to the congressional mandate of the Taiwan Relations Act to "maintain the capacity to resist the use of force against...Taiwan" and averred that "the United States takes these obligations very seriously." He explained:

> the President's *National Security Strategy*, published in September 2002, calls for "building a balance of power that favors freedom." Taiwan's evolution into a true multi-party democracy over the past decade is proof of the importance of America's commitment to Taiwan's defense. It strengthens

---

[105] Section 3303(b) of the TRA reads: "(1) Whenever the laws of the United States refer or relate to foreign countries, nations, states, governments, or similar entities, such terms shall include and such laws shall apply with respect to Taiwan."

[106] Kelly, "The Taiwan Relations Act: The Next Twenty-Five Years," p. 32. Kelly said, "The definition of one China is something that we could go on for much too long for this event. In my testimony, I made the point of our one China, and I really did not define it. I am not sure that I very easily could define it."

[107] Colin Powell, "Remarks at Asia Society Annual Dinner," June 10, 2002, at *www.state.gov/secretary/rm/2002/10983.htm*.

American resolve to see Taiwan's democracy grow
and prosper.[108]

That sums it up nicely.

---

[108] See "The Taiwan Relations Act: The Next 25 Years," prepared statement of Peter W.
Rodman, Assistant Secretary of Defense for International Security Affairs, before the
House International Relations Committee, April 21, 2004, p. 23, at *http://wwwa.house.
gov/international_relations/108/Rod042104.htm.* Rodman referred to U.S. National Security Council, *The National Security Strategy of the United States of America,* September 2002,
at *www.whitehouse.gov/nsc/nss.html.*

Appendix A

Rethinking "One China": A Fiction More Dangerous Than Useful?

Edited Transcript of a Heritage Foundation Symposium
February 26, 2004

JOHN J. TKACIK, JR.: We are honored this morning to have with us Congressmen Peter Deutsch of Florida, Joe Hoeffel of Pennsylvania, Dana Rohrabacher of California, and Bob Andrews of New Jersey, all members of the Congressional Taiwan Caucus and all deeply concerned about the implications of "one China" for the future of democracy in Asia. As you know, this promises to be the kick-off of a new policy debate looking at the so-called one-China policy. It will be a controversial, candid look at the issue, and, frankly, these questions need to be asked.

Is the "one China" policy still useful, or has it become a dangerous fiction? To start off the program, a number of members of the Congressional Taiwan Caucus have asked whether they might say a few words about this very important topic. Our first speaker this morning will be Congressman Peter Deutsch of Florida, a respected six-term Congressman who could be the next Senator from Florida.

REPRESENTATIVE PETER DEUTSCH: This is an opportunity to not just talk about an issue, but to try to influence an issue as well. The official position of the State Department is that there is a "one China" policy. That's fine, but there's only "one China" and there's really one Taiwan. I think that is a physical, historical reality.

There's a second part of the equation. One of the interesting things that most Americans—and I would venture to say even most Members of the United States House of Representatives and, for that matter, most members of the United States Senate—do not know is the history of Taiwan. Part of our participatory process in America is that I, through a constituent-oriented group in South Florida, had the opportunity when I was running for office to read books, talk to people, talk to experts, listen to both arguments.

There are people that will insist, historically, Taiwan is physically part of China, that they're both the same. In fact, the debate on the panel, to get to the basis of the issue, would almost be a historical debate, a factual debate that could bring in the emigration that occurred some 300 years ago, the cultural issues that occurred, the historical issues, the language issues.

I've always found it fascinating that there is this historical parallel between the United States' relationship to Great Britain and Taiwan's relationship to China. The amount of time when both countries were first settled is about the same. No one today would contemplate that the United States is part of Great Britain. Yet, obviously, people continue to talk about Taiwan as part of China. Just talking about it doesn't change the reality.

What happens now is that we have *that* as the official policy.

Let me also mention that one of the things that we as Americans, as American policymakers, are united about is, if the people of Taiwan chose as a democracy, in their sovereign right, to enter into union with another sovereign country, they have that ability. It has happened in history where countries, for reasons of their own national security, national defense, or national economic reasons, have created confederations, have created different entities. Technically, when the United States merged with Texas, Texas was a sovereign country. Texas decided to give up its sovereignty to become part of the United States in a vote of the people of Texas. I will tell you that that ultimately is the decision of the people of Taiwan.

But what is the role of the United States? The role of the United States is actually very dangerous when we consider Taiwan and China as China's decision to make. I think it's extraordinarily dangerous in an existential way, just in terms of military conflict that potentially could occur and which no one wants to see happen. But I also think, as the world's only superpower, we must ask: What are the values of the United States? What is our goal?

There is no more important value than our concept of freedom, of the rights of countries to determine their own futures. Taiwan is a functioning, transparent democracy today. For the United States to say to that country that "you're not really a country," which is effectively still the official policy of the United States of America—I will tell you that I believe the vast majority of Members of Congress, by our actions, have not supported the "official policy of the United States." The official policy is nuanced, as all of us are aware.

By comparison, look at what's going on in Haiti today where there is a conflict in terms of the ruler's legitimacy. The truth is that President Aristide's legitimacy today could be questioned at many levels. The Administration was just in total confusion about what to do. Comparing Haiti and Taiwan in terms of transparency and democracy is as clear as black and white.

Let me close by saying that if we call Taiwan "China," it doesn't make it China. If we call night day, it doesn't make it day. If we call black white, it doesn't make it white. Throughout world history and American history, we've seen that recognizing facts as they are is the correct way of dealing with international conflicts and international crises. Whenever we make the mistake of ignoring facts or wishing them away, there are tragic results. We need to define reality and then come to terms with the reality of the experience, the conditions, the economy, and the military situation in Taiwan, and to recognize that putting our heads in the sand doesn't change that reality.

This conference today and Taiwan's presidential election within the next couple of weeks obviously are historic opportunities for us and the Taiwanese people to participate in the shaping of reality, which is something that you can't do in China. That is something that I think is clear in the United States Congress for the vast majority of Members. They have been and continue to be supportive of the effort by the people of Taiwan to shape their own reality and, I think, will be in continued support of that effort.

MR. TKACIK: Our next speaker is Congressman Joe Hoeffel from Pennsylvania. Congressman Hoeffel has represented the 13th District of Pennsylvania for three terms, and is one of the newer members of the Congressional Taiwan Caucus. His focus in Congress has been especially on the global expansion of democracy, and he has had a special concern for democracy in Taiwan.

As a member of the House International Relations Committee, Congressman Hoeffel has thought very deeply about the issue of Taiwan. In January, he wrote a statement encouraging Taiwan to go ahead with the referendum to protest Chinese missiles and the Chinese missile threat. Please help me welcome Congressman Joe Hoeffel.

REPRESENTATIVE JOE HOEFFEL: Thank you for the invitation to talk about "one China." I particularly want to note the presence and the personal invitation of Jay Loo and his wife Helen Loo, who are constituents of mine and have helped to educate me about Taiwan.

The United States has a tremendously important role to play regarding the future of Taiwan, and that is, in the short run, to protect the status quo, to make sure that there is sufficient time for Taiwan and the People's Republic of China (the mainland) to try to figure out how to move forward in a peaceful way that reaches consensus. It won't be easy. We all know that. But the first thing we must say, as the United States Congress, is that we want to make sure that everyone knows that we will protect the status quo, that we will stand by Taiwan, that we meant what we said with the Taiwan Relations Act, and that we will continue to say to all parties concerned that the United States stands for the defense of Taiwan and will do whatever is necessary to protect that status quo.

The question in front of us today is: Where do we go from here, and what does our "one China" policy mean? What is the meaning of the referendum that President Chen Shui-bian advocates? What is the meaning of the aggressive measures taken by the People's Republic of China to position more missiles aimed at Taiwan? And what should America do?

There are two things about Taiwan I really like. One, it is now a flourishing multiparty democracy. It wasn't always multiparty, but it is now, and it is flourishing in large measure because of that political choice for freedom. Second, it is a flourishing and successful free-market economy. So the two things that this country holds most dear, Taiwan has undertaken with a remarkable level of success.

Let me say that there is, as Peter said, great support for the future of Taiwan on all sides in the Congress. Representative Rohrabacher and I serve on the House International Relations Committee. Many of us have traveled to Taiwan. I was there for one brief visit, but there is great support in the United States Congress for Taiwan.

In this context, I believe it is very appropriate for the referendum to move forward in March. That is certainly a defensive referendum: It is asking the people of Taiwan how to respond to this aggressive positioning of missiles in the People's Republic.

I think a long-term goal could be the unification of the People's Republic with the Republic of China, but I don't want to see that unification if it is requiring the assimilation of Taiwan into anything that looks like the current People's Republic of China. I want it to be the other way around. I want the flourishing multiparty democracy and the free-market economy of Taiwan to be what carries the day.

Let the mainland enjoy those freedoms. Let the government of the People's Republic reflect the openness and democracy that we see on Taiwan. That must be the goal of the United States. That is the only acceptable goal that we can have for the future of the Chinese people. We must stand in defense of Taiwan and in defense of the principles that we hold most dear as a nation:

personal freedom and democratic choice and social justice and human rights. Today, those principles are found on Taiwan, and that we must protect.

MR. TKACIK: Our next speaker is Congressman Dana Rohrabacher of California, representing California's scenic 46th District. Congressman Rohrabacher is literally one of the authors of the conservative movement. As a special assistant to President Reagan in the 1980s, he was one of President Reagan's speechwriters and had a pivotal role in the articulation of the Reagan Doctrine and in championing a strong national defense.

He is now the Chairman of the Space and Aeronautics Subcommittee. He is a senior member of the House International Relations Committee and has been a longtime advocate of the expansion of democracy throughout the world, especially in Asia, and has been a longtime fire bell in the night on the growing challenge of a rising China. Congressman Rohrabacher, thank you very much for coming.

REPRESENTATIVE DANA ROHRABACHER: Here in Washington, D.C., it's important for us to get straight to fundamentals. And what are the fundamentals that we need to understand when discussing issues such as the one we're talking about today? The most important one is that 250 years ago, the United States of America embarked on a new course for all humankind, that Americans here proclaimed their belief that all people have a right to determine their own destiny. We declared at the founding of this country, unlike any other country before it, that we believed all people everywhere have rights that are granted to them by God.

So when we are trying to determine what policies we will follow as a people today, we need to remind ourselves what our Founding Fathers believed and to act consistent with those values and beliefs. Those beliefs have made our world a prosperous world and a free world and a decent world for normal people, regular people to live in and in which to raise their families. But the rulers of nearly half of the rest of world still do not accept this.

In the 250 years from the time those ideas started springing, our ideals have had a tremendous impact on the world, and wherever you see freedom and justice and liberty in the world, it's because the people of the United States have tried to carry out these beliefs consistently rather than trying to compromise with whatever the threat was in that moment.

In World War II, we saw the German Nazis and the Japanese militarists believing that they had a right to dominate certain areas of the planet in the name of the Führer, or in the name of the Emperor, and that the conquered peoples of those areas had no right to object. We defeated that threat, and I'm very proud of the people of the United States. If it were not for the United States stepping up and opposing tyranny, the Japanese would still dominate the East with an iron fist, and the Nazis would still dominate the huge Western chunk of the planet with their iron boots. But they're not.

We did step forward, and our goal then should be our goal today: not that the United States dominates other countries, but that their peoples have a right to determine their own destinies through honest and free elections. Our goal with Taiwan should be no different: that the people of Taiwan, like people everywhere, have a right through free elections to determine their future, and if the people of Taiwan are threatened, we must step forward as we would step forward for anyone who is threatened by an alien dictatorship. The people of Taiwan will have the support of the United States government in ensuring that they can exercise their right to determine their own destiny. That's the fundamental.

Today, I'm sad to say, the greatest threat to freedom and stability on this planet is that a huge chunk of humanity on the mainland of China cannot enjoy their rights as human beings. There is a tyrannical power hostile to freedom and fundamental human rights that rules the mainland of China.

The people of Taiwan could do no greater service to all of us than to stand tall and strong and insist on their rights and to serve as a model for the mainland of China, to let the people of the mainland know that democracy is not just something for Europeans or Americans. Democracy and freedom are the birthright of all human beings. That thought is the most powerful force in Asia, because it is the one idea that will reform China and eliminate this last Communist threat, insofar as their brand of "Communism" is now merely a crude pseudo-legitimization of their right to rule China in the name of a discredited ideology.

We need solidarity among free people. That's the answer. The people of Taiwan are free, and the people of the mainland are not. Why is there a question about where America should stand? America should stand with the people of Taiwan who have gained freedom for themselves. I hope, when we face future challenges, that they will stand with America to ensure that other people who are struggling for their freedom, whether in Burma or Vietnam or North Korea or on the mainland of China, can obtain their freedom.

We do have bipartisan support here in the nation's capital for these ideals. When I talk about fundamentals, they are the fundamentals not just of the Republican Party or the Democratic Party, but of the United States of America. And Americans are on Taiwan's side.

MR. TKACIK: The congressmen have agreed to answer questions. When you ask a question, please state your name and your affiliation.

JENNIE LIN: I am Jennie Lin, and I am a concerned citizen. Some of you have said that if China were today to enjoy a multiparty system, political democracy, and free economy, then we could talk about reunification. Of course, China does not enjoy that ideal democratic society that you talked about, but I am curious why there is a need for reunification between Taiwan and China any more than there might be one for the British and the United States, which share the same political ideology?

REPRESENTATIVE HOEFFEL: I think that is probably the best long-range goal to strive for. Independence for Taiwan is another option. I think it would be very hard to achieve independence for Taiwan in the current circumstance, so I think our short-term goal as the United States should be to protect the status quo, defend Taiwan, and be clear about what we want to see.

What I want to see is the democracy and free-market economy that are flourishing in Taiwan spread to the mainland and spread throughout Asia. I don't think Congress should ever stand in the way of some alternative future for Taiwan as long as it's peaceful and the Taiwanese people get to choose. The right of self-determination, of course, is fundamental.

CHARLES SNYDER: Charles Snyder, Washington correspondent of the *Taipei Times*. We understand that the congressional leadership is somewhat averse at this time to allowing a resolution supporting a referendum in Taiwan and a strong pro-Taiwan referendum, but where does that stand? Do you think that, in fact, there should be some sort of resolution before the March 20 election, and do you think it's possible?

REPRESENTATIVE DEUTSCH: Let me respond. I'd be happy to hear Dana's response as well, because I think we're on the same side of the issue but against the leadership.

There have been some very, very strong supporters of the self-determination of Taiwan across the ideological spectrum of the United States Congress: liberal, conservative, moderate, progressive, and everything else. Tom Delay has been a real leader, as many of you well know. I've spoken to him about it. My staff and his staff have interacted, as we have on many issues. I think his initial reaction was to do exactly what you're describing, and I've been very supportive of that and I'm still supportive of it.

I have a lot of respect for Congressman DeLay, particularly on this and several other issues—although we disagree on probably 75 to 95 percent of the issues. But this is an issue where he and I see eye-to-eye. My personal perspective is that his support for Taiwan is only overweighed by his desire not to hurt the President.

I think, in the political context, the Administration has weighed in extraordinarily heavily to prevent the resolution from being adopted. It's been drafted, as you are aware, and has extraordinarily bipartisan support. The numbers in the House would probably be close to unanimous if it were actually on the floor of the House. But what is clear at this point, at least from as recently as yesterday, is that it will not come up between now and the election, which I think is unfortunate.

The people of Taiwan should not view that in any negative sense at all. The Congress has been close to universal in a position of support of the referendum, as has been shown by cosponsorship and letters to that effect, so it should be clear to the people of Taiwan, where I know that our actions in Congress do have an effect. What we say in Congress is on the front page of the papers in Taiwan and on television and radio. I'm curious about Dana's response.

REPRESENTATIVE ROHRABACHER: First and foremost, I believe that Taiwanese President Chen Shui-bian's idea of challenging the mainland to have a demilitarized buffer zone was a good idea. Fundamentally, it created a debate and brought up an issue that was important because it reflected the values of people on both sides of the Strait, so I think President Chen had a good idea there.

In terms of the referendum, if the people want to have a vote on an issue, they should have a vote on the issue. Anyone who raises questions about it or tries to think that this is something that concerns anyone else demonstrates a lack of understanding of the fundamentals. The people of Taiwan can vote on whatever they want to vote on, and let's hope that some day the people of mainland China will be able to vote on what they want to vote on too.

REPRESENTATIVE HOEFFEL: I agree with my colleagues—two smart men here.

JAY CHEN (Central News Agency, Taipei): I have a comment about the Bush Administration's objection to the referendum. It's very unfortunate, and it's inconsistent with the values that you Congressmen mentioned, the democratic values of self-determination; but it's self-defeating, too, when the Bush team interferes in the domestic politics of Taiwan this way, because it encourages the KMT [Kuomintang Party] and PFP [People First Party] people to try to boycott the referendum. I just wish the Congress could have been stronger in expressing its support for that referendum.

REPRESENTATIVE DEUTSCH: Dana and I worked very closely on this, and I think his response was absolutely accurate. I can be harsher to the Administration and the Republican leadership than, obviously, he can, but I want this to be somewhat of a dialogue.

I think it is important to understand that there is close to unanimity on a congressional level. It's not 100 percent, probably maybe 90 percent or 80 percent, but it's a huge consensus point in Congress—exactly what you're saying. In a sense, we're struggling, or I'm struggling, with what else to do. I've been on television. I've taped things. I've written things directly to the people of Taiwan about this. I know some of my other colleagues have as well.

So I would almost say that the Administration's actions have had a direct effect in Taiwan on how people perceive both the referendum and the presidential election. I agree with you; we shouldn't be trying to influence it, but the reality is, we have. Whether we want to or not, we in fact already have influenced what's going on in Taiwan by [U.S. Secretary of State] Colin Powell's statements and by the Administration's actions. What else can we do? I don't know if we can do very much else.

REPRESENTATIVE HOEFFEL: If I can add to what Peter said, I agree with his comments. We ought to have that vote in order to express the solidarity of Congress with the right of the people of Taiwan to vote on a referendum. As Dana has said, they certainly have that right.

I think the Bush Administration made a mistake. They have weighed in, I believe, on the wrong side of this issue, and I would like to see Congress weigh in with our support for the right of the Taiwanese people to have this vote.

REPRESENTATIVE DEUTSCH: When I look back on 12 years that I've been in the United States Congress, I am not prouder of any other thing that I did than when I took a leadership role among a group of Congressmen and Congresswomen when the Chinese threatened the island of Taiwan in 1996 and President Clinton was not as active as he could have been. We passed almost a unanimous resolution of support in terms of reaffirming our commitment to put American men and women in harm's way to defend the obligations under the laws that we have for the defense of Taiwan, and it pushed the Administration to act. That's something that, really, we can have a role in.

REPRESENTATIVE ROHRABACHER: I, of course, am totally supportive of having a vote in support of the people of Taiwan's right to have a vote, but this doesn't have anything to do with the Bush Administration or the Clinton Administration. This has everything to do with the financial establishment pressuring the government to forget our values and to forget our principles so they can pursue a profit on the mainland of China. That's all it's about.

America is about more than just a place where people came to make money. I think people being able to make a profit's a good idea, but simply to encourage American firms to invest in another country in order to make a profit is not the ultimate goal of American foreign policy and shouldn't be.

The ultimate goal of American foreign policy should be establishing relationships with other free people in different parts of the world to try to further those ideals and make it a better world. I don't think that backing down to thugs and dictators in order to somehow make it easier for people to make money is a good idea. It gives a wrong impression.

This has been a problem through Republican and Democratic Administrations. I've been here 16 years now, and it's happened ever since Tiananmen Square. When I worked with Ronald Reagan, it looked like China was going to be able to evolve out of its dictatorship; but on June 4, 1989, at Tiananmen Square, there was a major reversal. At that point, there should have been no excuse for us to continue the type of positive relationship that we've had with those people who rule China with an iron fist.

So it's been a bipartisan mistake as well. We've got people in both parties who are trying to work on both sides of this issue.

I-SHON WEN: My name is I-Shon Wen. I come from Baltimore, a member of the Taiwanese/American Association chapter. Is it true that the American Institute in Taiwan in Kaohsiung is already preparing for withdrawal of unnecessary family members back to the United States because the U.S. opposes a Taiwan referendum?

REPRESENTATIVE DEUTSCH: I don't think this whole issue of us saying not to go through with the referendum is important. What you have is a really competitive election campaign in Taiwan. In American presidential elections, there have been altered photographs. There are all sorts of things going on, and it's hard to filter out the truth.

But I think the truth is, this support that exists for Taiwan and the support of the referendum is overwhelming in terms of the center of the country and, in fact, the center of the Congress. That's the fact. How do you express that fact? The easiest way would be by a resolution that passed 400 to 10 or something like that. That's not going to take place.

REPRESENTATIVE ROHRABACHER: Let me state very clearly for the people of Taiwan: Whatever way they vote in this referendum will in no way determine whether or not the United States stays and has a presence in Taiwan. There is no threat to them from the people of the United States or the government of the United States right now. This Administration may be expressing some opposition or some hesitation about the referendum, but if there is a referendum in Taiwan, our presence will continue no matter what happens in that referendum.

ARTHUR WALDRON: I'm Arthur Waldron from the University of Pennsylvania, and I want to thank the Congressmen for their very forthright and clear-eyed assessment of the real situation.

If it is the case that you cannot actually have a vote on the floor of the Congress on a resolution supporting a Taiwan referendum, would it be possible to develop some sort of a petition or list of Congressmen, and perhaps other people, who in fact support this position that would not be an official U.S. government document? Gather the names of the people who would vote in the House and the Senate, maybe get names from elsewhere, and then give this some publicity before the election?

There's no question that the message that the people of Taiwan are getting is very confusing, and that's largely owing to media distortion there and to confusion about what our Administration said. So I think that one thing that might come out of this meeting would be some sort of a petition or a public statement. I would strongly suggest that.

REPRESENTATIVE DEUTSCH: I would agree with you completely. I think that we probably, through the three of us and through some of the constituent groups that are based here, could get in the high 300s Members signing on a letter to the people of Taiwan. I don't think that would be a problem. It's just a logistical thing. I'm willing to put my time in, and I'm sure my colleagues are as well. So, hopefully, that will happen.

MR. TKACIK: From the First District of New Jersey, Congressman Bob Andrews is another staunch advocate of expanding democracy throughout the world. Again, the issue of democracy in Taiwan is one of those issues where liberals and conservatives agree wholeheartedly. Ladies and gentlemen, please welcome Congressman Bob Andrews of New Jersey.

REPRESENTATIVE ROBERT ANDREWS: We meet at a time that is crucial for the foreign policy of a great nation, a time when people's will and principle will be tested, and whether or not that country's relatively new experiment in democracy will thrive or perish. The country that I speak about is not Taiwan. It is the United States of America. We will be measured by how we treat brother and sister democracies in the world.

American foreign policy, in my view, gets in trouble when we make one or both of two fundamental mistakes—and I think we're making both of these fundamental mistakes in our assessment of Taiwan's place in the world. The first mistake is to misapprehend evolving dynamics of history. Wayne Gretzky, the great hockey player, once said that great hockey players don't know where the puck is; they only know where the puck's going. Too often, we've been blind to the dynamics and forces of the world and have not seen where things were going.

I would give you the example of our behavior in Iran and Iraq in the 1970s and the 1980s. In the 1970s, our supportive posture toward the Shah of Iran was premised upon the argument that the Soviet threat was the greatest threat to American existence in the future and that, almost irrespective of an ally's conduct or an ally's standards, we should embrace anyone who is hostile to the Soviet Union as an ally of the United States. We fully embraced the Peacock Throne, the Shah of Iran, and sowed seeds of great antipathy among the Iranian people, which led to the 1979 toppling of the Shah, the violent revolution, the seizing of the American hostages, and a sorry history that we live with the remnants of to this day. One of the major issues we face in this country is trying to contain weapons of mass destruction that certainly exist in Iran.

We failed to understand the dynamic of another major threat looming in the horizon. It was the antipathy of a billion Muslims and the hatred that might breed toward the United States. We also failed to see the inevitable unraveling of the Soviet Union that our own country's wise policies, frankly initiated by President Reagan, brought to a head.

In Iraq in the 1980s, we made a similar mistake. Because we were so mortified by the evolution of the fundamentalist government in Iran, we defined anyone who opposed that government as our ally, and we embraced as a quasi-ally in the 1980s a leader named Saddam Hussein. We assisted him in his efforts to fight a bloody, seemingly pointless 10-year war against his Iranian neighbors. We enriched him, we armed him, we emboldened him, and we lived until a year ago with the consequences of that decision.

Due to what I believe is the wise and good judgment of another President, George W. Bush, the right decision was made to remove Saddam Hussein from power—one for which I voted in 2002 and for which I would vote eagerly again.

What we should learn from this is that, if we ignore larger dynamics to embrace short-term tactics, we do so at our own peril. The larger dynamic that we are ignoring in Asia is the irrepressible urge for freedom. The short-term tactic that we are embracing is the notion that very short-term tactics, like return on this quarter's balance sheet for cheap imports, justifies embracing a regime that is callous, inhumane, and disrespectful of human rights—not just human rights for people within its own country, but human rights for people around the world.

We are failing to see that the main dynamic in Asia is not the burgeoning growth of the economy of the PRC. It is the unyielding desire of people in Asia for freedom, self-respect, and self determination. We are misreading this historical dynamic.

The second mistake that we frequently make is to forget our own history, to confuse means with ends. I believe we made such a mistake in our years of support for the apartheid regimes in South Africa, where we confused the means of developing a stable trading partner with the end of opposing the repression of and discrimination against human beings because of the color of their skin. It took a long time for this country to change our policy, but change it we did, and humankind all over the world enjoys the fruits of that change.

Nelson Mandela, who sat in a prison cell the first day that I became a United States Congressman, addressed a joint session of the United States Congress from the podium of the House of Representatives as the president of South Africa just a few years later. This happened with relatively little bloodshed, relatively little violence. It was a peaceful resolution because America remembered that our adherence and commitment to our own history is a history of liberation. It is a history of recognition that people of all walks of life from all backgrounds are entitled to the basic dignity of human life: the right to raise their children as they see fit, the right to choose their own leaders, the right to be free from repressive government.

This is our heritage. It is our special place in human history. And when we forget it, we do so at our own peril.

The United States' relationship with Taiwan and the consequences of that relationship for our relationship with the People's Republic of China is as much about us as it is about Taiwan. What should we do?

We should be unequivocal in our support for freedom. We should do so not simply because it is the right thing for the people of Taiwan, for the 23 million people who live in Taiwan; we should do so because it's the right thing for us. America's security interests are always advanced when democracy spreads.

I'm not a very good student of history—although I did read Dr. Ross Terrill's book when I was in college, and I'm glad that I did. It was one of my textbooks. But I can't think of one instance in the history of the world where one democracy attacked another one; at least in modern times, I can't think of one instance. Democrats don't attack democrats. I'm not talking about John Kerry and John Edwards here. I'm talking about democrats with a small "d."

And I think I know why. The first thing I did this morning when I got up was to awaken my daughters, who are 11 years old and nine years old, and get them started on their way to school. There are very few circumstances under which I would choose to send either of my precious children off to fight a war. There are some, but there are very few. I would always regard it as a last resort, as an absolutely necessary choice to make, and I think moms and dads all over the world, from all different faiths and all different backgrounds, fundamentally share that view. If you get the right to vote on what your country's going to do, you look at war as a last resort, aggression as a last resort. That is why we are safer when democracy spreads and freedom spreads.

There's much talk in our history of a "one China" policy. I think we should replace our "one China" policy with a "higher principle" policy, and the higher principle should be "freedom for everyone wherever it is possible." America should be the moving force in creating that freedom for everyone wherever it is possible.

What does this mean in the immediate context? It means the Administration and the Congress should send a clear and unmistakable symbol that what will happen within a month in Taiwan is something we support and embrace. A popular will being expressed through a popular referendum is right. It is consistent with American values, and there should be no ambiguity as to where we stand on that.

I have introduced in the House, November 21 of last year, House Resolution 340, which states that view, and I'm urging my Republican and Democratic colleagues to join with me so it can be put on the House floor prior to the referendum, so we can send that signal as Republicans and Democrats, liberals and conservatives.

The second thing we should do is be unwavering in our commitment to extend, where necessary, defensive military technology to the government of Taiwan. I don't believe that anyone should preserve freedom by half measures or on the cheap. When you have a menacing neighbor who is building its offensive capacities methodically, you need to build your defensive capacities methodically. I've long favored the extension of the Aegis radar technology to the people of Taiwan so they can defend themselves against the growing threat across the Taiwan Strait with respect to the ballistic missiles held by the PRC.

Third, I believe that the most important gain that we can make toward democracy in the PRC is to be a staunch friend of democracy in Taiwan. I think democracy is what I would call a positive

epidemic. Some of you may have read Malcolm Gladwell's delight-
ful book called *The Tipping Point*.[1] If you haven't, I recommend
that you do. It's a wonderful story about how social behavior can
behave the way disease does. The same way a disease is a negative
epidemic that spreads throughout a society or a community, so
can positive behavioral traits.

I think democracy can spread in such a way. It's one of the reasons I'm in support of what we're doing in Iraq, because the possibility of 24 million Iraqis choosing their leaders and writing their
constitution and seeing and raising their children and living their
lives as they see fit is an epidemic I think can spread to Saudi Arabia and Syria and Iran and the rest of that region. It's one of the
reasons why some of the so-called moderate Arab leaders aren't so
enthusiastic about what we're doing, because they don't want to
see this tide rolling across their borders into their own country.

One of the places where democracy is most precious and most
practiced in Asia is Taiwan. We should validate and value that precious practice. I believe that the most effective way to ensure a
peaceful evolution of the PRC toward that of a peaceful and democratic trading partner, and away from that of a bellicose and
emerging military superpower, is for us to support and revere the
democracy that sits at the PRC's doorstep. It is the right thing to
do for the United States, not simply the right thing to do for the
people of Taiwan.

So I conclude where I began. This is about our history. I live
eight miles from Independence Hall in Philadelphia, a place
where some incredibly visionary men wrote a document—wrote
a series of documents, actually—which have given life and a wonderful gift and blessing to us generations later.

At the time this young country was struggling for its independence, a great world power stepped forward for reasons of some self-
interest and some nobility and assisted the United States in achieving that dream of independence and freedom. It's one of the

---

[1] Malcolm Gladwell, *The Tipping Point: How Little Things Can Make a Big Difference*
(Boston, Back Bay Books, 2002).

reasons why, until very recent years, the relationship between France and the United States was such a positive and good one. We are fortunate that the French stepped forward and served the cause of liberty 225 years ago, despite their reluctance to do so 12 months ago.

The United States is a far more powerful force in the world today than France was in 1775, and Taiwan is a far weaker presence than the colonies were in 1775. That's all the more reason why we should read our own history, follow our own principles, support this referendum in March but, more important, support the continuing march of freedom and progress in Taiwan so that it may spread to all of the people who live in Asia, so that it may benefit all of the people who live in the rest of the world.

MR. TKACIK: The Congressman has graciously offered to answer one or two questions before we move on. Jay Chen of Central News Agency in Taipei.

JAY CHEN: Congressman, you made an eloquent speech about the need for the United States to support democracy throughout the world, but we have a situation in the Taiwan Strait. On the one hand, there seems to be a growing aspiration for a future in Taiwan independent of the mainland. On the other hand, there's no denying the growth of the People's Republic of China. How realistic is it, therefore, of any U.S. Administration supporting an independent Taiwan?

REPRESENTATIVE ANDREWS: It is not only realistic; it is essential. If you adopt a worldview that says that we should choose means over ends, tactics over principles, then you adopt a worldview that says these Taiwanese people keep wanting to have elections and referenda and a constitution and civil rights, and that's very inconvenient because it embarrasses us in our trade relations and our diplomatic relations with the much larger country across the Strait.

That would be a huge mistake for the United States to choose short-term accommodation over long-term interest. If the economy of the PRC grows in the next 20 years at the pace at which it's grown in the last 20 years, in real-dollar military terms, 20 years from today, the Chinese military establishment will be about twice as large as the U.S. military establishment is today, plane for plane, missile for missile, ship for ship.

And the PRC will not have to choose between guns and butter. My analysis assumes that the percentage of the PRC's GDP devoted to defense stays the same. It is such a vast and growing pie that would make such a thing possible.

I don't want us in 20 years to be facing a global superpower that can call five times as many men and women to arms as we can, based on population, with a military establishment twice the size ours is today in real-dollar terms. I don't want to be living in that world. It is very much in our interest to do what we can to persuade the PRC's path of development away from military superpower confrontation and toward democracy.

I think the biggest mistake that we could make is to say to the leaders of the PRC that we're timid about challenging their direction. I think they will read timidity as weakness, and they will exploit weakness as an invitation to compete with us militarily. It's a competition I think we'd win, but it's one I do not want to have.

You make a huge mistake in any relationship if you start out trying to persuade someone by being weak rather than being strong. We should be strong without being bellicose, without being provocative, without being negative; but we should be strong. If we say to the PRC that we're going to support this referendum, and we're going to provide for the self-defense of Taiwan, and we're going to support Taiwan's involvement in the World Health Organization and other international organizations, this will be very unpopular in Beijing, but it will send a message of strength and clarity that I believe will have a positive influence in the evolution of that country.

AMBASSADOR HARVEY FELDMAN: My name is Harvey Feldman, a former Foreign Service officer. I'm now Senior Fellow in the Asian Studies Center here at The Heritage Foundation, and I've been thinking about "one China" for a long time.

I'd like to begin with just a few words about what this "one China" policy is, because nobody's yet said what it is. But first, I want to tell you what the PRC's "one China" policy is. Their policy's very, very simple: There's only one China in the world. Taiwan is part of that one China. The legal government and the only legal government and the only legal representative of that one China is the government of the People's Republic in Beijing.

That's not the U.S. policy, but a lot of people seem to think that it is also the U.S. policy, that we have agreed that Taiwan is part of China. In point of fact, we have never done so.

Very simply put, the U.S. "one China" policy is that we will have diplomatic relations only with the People's Republic of China, but that we will have all manner of other cultural, commercial, and very extensive defense relationships with the Republic of China on Taiwan. You have to understand this distinction. We have never said that we regard Taiwan as part of the People's Republic of China.

Our panel will go over in more detail how we got to this point and, I hope, will talk about how we move beyond it. In a world in which Nauru, with a population of 8,000, is a member of the United Nations and Taiwan, with its 23-plus million people, is not only not a member of the United Nations, but a bunch of countries around the world consider that it is not even a state—this is a very strange and absurd world, and any kind of principle that would lock that in is a very strange and absurd principle.

We're going to begin with Arthur Waldron. Arthur is the Lauder Professor of International Relations at the University of Pennsylvania. He's written many, many books. One of my favorites is *The Great Wall of China: From History to Myth*.[2]

ARTHUR WALDRON: Thank you very much, Harvey, for clarifying this issue of what we mean by "one China." I think it's absolutely essential that people understand what the PRC means by "one China"—namely, that Taiwan is part of China—and what we mean

---

[2] Arthur Waldron, *The Great Wall of China: From History to Myth* (Cambridge, UK: Cambridge University Press, reprint 1992).

by it, which is that we can only recognize one government of China, but we do not recognize that Taiwan is part of China. I think that's very important to stress.

I think it's fair to say that the situation we're in now had its origins in the 1970s, which was an unusual era. This was a time when the United States was being defeated in Vietnam; when confidence in American institutions, in freedom and so forth, was ebbing; when even so eminent a person as Daniel Patrick Moynihan opined that democracy was something that could only be enjoyed by a handful of states of Northern European heritage.

At that time of weakness, Henry Kissinger and Richard Nixon decided that it was no longer possible, given the great Soviet threat, to face that threat alone, even with NATO. They assumed that the Soviet Union was permanent. They assumed that the China of Mao Zedong was also permanent, that this was the sort of final historical incarnation of Chinese civilization after hundred years of false starts.

They also assumed that the obstacle to forming a new, stable, and balanced constellation of China and the U.S. balancing the Soviet Union was Taiwan. They assumed, as they saw South Vietnam going down the drain, that, like South Vietnam, Taiwan was in effect an American client state. Its government was unrepresentative of the people who lived on the island. It was a dictatorship, and it was assumed that if we were to cut relations with the island, the blow administered would be such as to cause, after a decent interval, the leadership—Chiang Kai-shek or his successors—to reach over the heads of the people of Taiwan and make an agreement with the government of the People's Republic of China, thereby eliminating this issue, this constant annoyance of Taiwan.

There was so much confidence in this—what I call "Plan A"—that no other plan was talked about.

Kissinger in his memoirs has a wonderful passage where he talks about the day he was leaving for China and he ran into James Shen, who was the ROC ambassador. Kissinger said—you can almost visualize the crocodile tears flowing down his face—that no government less deserved what was about to happen to it than that of Taiwan. What exactly was about to happen to it?

It was particularly painful meeting with Ambassador Shen because Kissinger "knew that before long this esoteric discussion of UN procedural maneuvres would be overtaken by more elemental events."[3] There's no question that like his hero, Prince Metternich, Kissinger imagined that he was recasting the world and creating stability.

That was 25 years ago. Suppose now that Henry Kissinger had gone to sleep at some point in the 1970s and then woke up today, let us say in this room. I think he would be baffled. He would say, "What is this Taiwan that you are talking about? Surely, it joined China round about 1983 at the latest. What's going on?" We would then have to explain the things that rendered his calculations incorrect.

First, the Soviet Union turned out not to be permanent.

Second, Chairman Mao's China quickly disappeared following Mao's death. It didn't disappear as a dictatorship, but the way that China looked was utterly transformed. However—and I think that this is a key point about China—the China that exists today, despite all of the changes that have occurred, is still politically rigid, and there is no sign that I can discern of any forward movement on the political side.

Again, this is something of which Prince Metternich would approve. However, if I can appose to Prince Metternich Edmund Burke, Burke once said, "A state without the means of some change is without the means of its conservation." I think that that is correct. In other words, until the PRC develops some way to adjust and change, it's not going to be able to survive.

The third most important change was that Taiwan failed to do what it was supposed to do under "Plan A." Instead, it democratized, and this was entirely unexpected. I'm told by people who know the State Department archives that there were no planning papers, no consideration whatsoever of any outcome except one in which the exiled government in Taiwan made terms over the heads of the people of Taiwan. That's how confident we were.

---

[3] Henry Kissinger, *White House Years* (Boston: Little, Brown, 1979), p. 733.

In the business of strategy—and I was a Professor of Strategy at the Naval War College for a number of years—that is not called "strategic analysis." That's called scripting. It's a very common error that, instead of thinking about all the different things that might happen, you say, "This is what's going to happen. We're going to do this, then they're going to do that." And if the other actors fail to read their lines properly, then you're in big trouble.

This has now landed us in a position where we have a situation that was intended to be transitional, but which has become permanent or seemingly permanent and is putting down ever-deeper roots as democracy becomes stronger in Taiwan and as the legitimacy of the government there becomes undeniable, even as the illegitimacy of the government in PRC also becomes clear.

So "Plan A" has failed, although there are people in this town and in China who are still carrying the torch for "Plan A." But I think the time has long passed for us to think about "Plan B." In other words, how are we going to deal with reality?

To do this, I should add, we are severely constrained by the fact that we have played this game according to a script, and we have given away all sorts of cards that we might have played quite effectively. Thus, if Kissinger had paid more attention to that discussion with James Shen about the U.N., it's conceivable that the Republic of China would still be in the U.N. and that a lot of these issues of "what do you do with a state that is very important to the world economy, which is critical strategically, if it fails to do what you expected?" could have been avoided.

You can engage in denial, and that's really what we do. If you look in the CIA *World Factbook*[4] and you look up North Korea, underneath the title it says "official name," and it will say "Democratic People's Republic of Korea" even though we don't recognize it. If you look up Taiwan in the CIA *World Factbook*, it will say "Taiwan," and then it will say, "official name"—and it says "none."

---

[4]U.S. Central Intelligence Agency, *The World Factbook 2003*, weekly updates available at *www.cia.gov/cia/publications/factbook/*. North Korea is at *www.cia.gov/cia/publications/factbook/geos/kn.html*; for some unknown reason, Taiwan's entry is at the *end* of the alphabetical listing at *www.cia.gov/cia/publications/factbook/geos/tw.html*.

That's simply not a fact. There *is* an official name. What are we doing giving our CIA people a reference book that misleads them about what the place calls itself? We're engaging in make-believe, just as we did with the Nationalist regime there.

Some people will say that China policy must be based on some necessary myths. Maybe to some it makes sense to base policies on myths, but I would argue that if you're going to have a good policy, it ought to be based on realities, and the realities simply do not correspond to the ones that were anticipated in the '70s.

The Soviet Union has disappeared and with it the restraint that its threat from the north posed to China. China has begun to change and is certainly going to continue to change, but as I remarked, this transition is directionless. In other words, all sorts of forces are on the loose in China, but no one inside China, or outside, can say what the desired end state is.

Deng Xiaoping used to say, "We'll cross the river by feeling the stones under our feet." That may or may not be a good way to cross the river, but the question you want to ask is, "Why are we crossing the river? What's on the other side? Why should we go there?" No one can tell us what China is going to look like in 10 years or 20 or 30 years, although I can assure you it will look different.

We have to come to terms with the fact that Taiwan is not going to go away. In fact, quite the opposite: It's my own belief that, unless the island is betrayed by somebody who does not consult the people, if the people are allowed to choose, it's not going to go away and that there will be, from now on and indefinitely, always an elected parliament and an elected president in Taipei.

How long is there going to be a Politburo in Beijing? I think that that has a more limited life expectancy than the democracy in Taiwan. In Chinese there's the doctrine of the "rectification of names"—to use the right names for things—to describe things as they really are.

We don't have time and I don't have the wisdom to describe what our "Plan B" should be, but I can say that, first of all, it has to deal concretely with the continuing existence of Taiwan as a democracy. It has to embrace and support democracy, because democracy is a value that we believe in and it's good for the world.

Instead of being based on necessary myths, it's time for us to throw off the shackles of all of the basically false language that we have used to describe the relationship between China and Taiwan and the United States: Throw off the shackles of that language, "rectify names," begin calling things what they really are, and then have an honest and open discussion.

AMBASSADOR FELDMAN: I ran the task force in the State Department on dual representation the year we tried to preserve Taiwan's membership, saying, "Yes, the PRC should come in, but Taiwan should not be expelled." It was like running a race where the coach, Dr. Kissinger, says, "The other team gets to start first, and after a while you can start."

I started running around the track, and the coach says, "You need a weight belt." Then he attached the weight belt, and I ran some more and caught up again. Meanwhile, he went off to Beijing and, in fact, was in Beijing conferring with Zhou Enlai the day of the vote, and we lost that vote very, very narrowly: 53–55–15. It's a number I will always remember.

Our second speaker is Tom Donnelly, Resident Fellow in National Security at the American Enterprise Institute. He also moonlights as an adjunct faculty member at Syracuse University, where he teaches national security strategy. He's written lots of books, and a forthcoming book, *Operation Iraqi Freedom: A Strategic Assessment*,[5] should be a best seller.

THOMAS DONNELLY: I'd like to carry the story forward, as it were, over the last couple of years and make an argument that the problems of the "one China" policy are particularly critical in the post-9/11 era and particularly dangerous within the context of the so-called Bush Doctrine, recognizing that the Bush Doctrine

---

[5] Thomas Donnelly, *Operation Iraqi Freedom: A Strategic Assessment* (Washington, D.C.: AEI Press, 2004).

is a work in progress, still being defined in many ways. The one really critical problem for this doctrine is how to deal with the legacy of the "one China" problem.

It's worth making an analogy between national security strategies and the skin of a snake, in that snakeskins are good for a season, but if you cannot shed them, you cannot grow. The "one China" policy, as I regard it, was perhaps once supple and smooth back in the days of the 1970s, but it is certainly a dry crust, maybe a scab, on the healthy American approach to strategy-making today.

We've had a hard time making a coherent national security strategy since the end of the Cold War. There have been partisans and analysts on all sides of the political equation who have tried to repair the crumbling ideas of the past. But certainly in the wake of September 11, we understand that the two traditional approaches of the past—certainly the billiard-ball balance-of-power realism represented by Kissinger—are no longer sufficient.

The rhetoric of strategic competition, which was the one generally innovative and interesting point that the President had made during the campaign, was pretty unceremoniously, dramatically, and immediately thrown out the window. It does seem very curious in retrospect, but Secretary of Defense Don Rumsfeld's Pentagon was immediately thrust into the shadows and Secretary of State Colin Powell stepped forward to seize the reins of policymaking, which was no doubt a great relief to the established bureaucracy.

The April 1, 2001, EP–3 reconnaissance aircraft incident brought back all the traditional language about dealing with the People's Republic and re-establishing the relationship, which is more often regarded as an end in itself rather than a means to achieving American goals within the bureaucratic establishment. The White House in particular wanted to suggest that we did not want to escalate the crisis, and the President himself mentioned "the expressed desire of both our countries for better relations."[6]

---

[6]The White House, Office of the Press Secretary, "Statement by the President on American Plane and Crew in China," April 2, 2001, at *www.whitehouse.gov/news/releases/2001/04/20010402-2.html.*

That's a quote that could have come from pretty much any President at any time from 1970 up until that moment.

The longer the incident went unresolved, the more humiliating the crisis became. The Chinese were pretty truculent about giving our people back, had a great time ripping the EP-3 apart to see what they could get out of it. And, of course, on the recommendation of Secretary Powell, we were keeping our powder dry and our mouths shut.

The resolution of the crisis was, at least in rhetorical terms, an apology for the incident, very carefully couched to say that "what we really did regret was the loss of the Chinese pilot's life." The practical propaganda and political impact of it was certainly understood—and played—in China and in the region as an American apology.

And the problem didn't even end there, because that provided a window to reassert that Chinese Communist Party General Secretary Jiang Zemin had intervened mightily in the internal struggle between the moderates and the hardliners in the Chinese government and, by his heroic efforts, walked us back from the brink of war and was due a favor which, in particular, meant that we had to scale back impending arms sales to Taiwan. That is always the punch line.

Luckily, the President didn't quite feel the same sense of debt toward Jiang Zemin, and about three weeks later, he made the famous gaffe—"gaffe" in Washington means you're telling the truth—that the United States would do "whatever it takes"[7] to defend Taiwan. Indeed, even more salient was that he used the term that the United States has an "obligation" to defend Taiwan.

Again, the mandarins of the status quo, who had been enjoying a moment of justification and a feeling of renewal, immediately went into meltdown mode. Massachusetts Senator John Kerry, who was actually one of the first to leap to the microphones and defend

---

[7] See transcript of President Bush's remarks on "Good Morning, America," April 25, 2001, at *http://abcnews.go.com/sections/GMA/GoodMorningAmerica/GMA010425Bush_100days.html.*

the conventional wisdom in terms that preserved his options, lamented the implications of this change, which he said were serious, served neither American interests nor Taiwan's. Because he understood the danger of committing to the defense of Taiwan, he was reluctant to do so and, most curiously, acted as though he'd never thought about the prospect that China might actually attack Taiwan. This seemed to be an entirely new idea to him.[8]

To be fair to the early Bush Administration, there was meant to be a method in their maddening inconsistencies in that, as good realists, their view was that the United States needed to preserve its freedom of action above all other precepts and policy and annoying details like political principles and political ideology.

Like Arthur, I too came equipped with a Metternich reference. I am reminded that there is a difference of opinion over who Henry Kissinger's real antecedents are; whether they be Talleyrand, Bismarck, or Metternich is probably the source for many future academic conferences. But I think we can say with some confidence that neither Alexander Hamilton nor Thomas Jefferson nor any other American strategist or statesman can be seen as an appropriate Kissingerian antecedent.

For a very long time, the establishment has embraced "one China" for its supposed "strategic ambiguity." For these folks, the fact that it's an obvious fiction is a plus-factor rather than a minus-factor. But in a post-9/11 world, this is a huge problem.

Nor will I reiterate the argument that says the world has changed since September 11, but I would like to at least stipulate that, certainly, the President believes that the world has changed. So far, this is a process rather than a fully developed doctrine.

Even the President's National Security Strategy[9] of 2002 is more a statement of goals than a genuine "how to" sort of strategy. Yet there are implications that one can extract and that one can

---

[8] See U.S. Department of State news release, "Text: Kerry Says U.S. Not Obligated to Defend Taiwan from Attacks (Sen. Kerry's speech on President Bush's remarks)," April 25, 2001, at *http://usinfo.org/USIA/usinfo.state.gov/regional/ea/uschina/taikerry.htm.*

[9] The White House, *The National Security Strategy of the United States of America*, September 2002, at *www.whitehouse.gov/nsc/nss.html.*

increasingly see played out as the doctrine becomes more fully developed. It has become the basis for American policy in the world.

I would argue that there are essentially two essential tenets that one can extract from the Bush Doctrine. First of all is that the United States wishes to remain the preeminent power in the world. That requires us to do a couple of things. It requires us to maintain the relatively peaceful state of play among the world's great powers in Europe, the greater Middle East, and in East Asia, and it also requires us to prevent terrorists, rogue regimes, and other lesser powers from acquiring weapons of mass destruction—which will confound the normal assessments of power and strategy—that they would otherwise obtain.

That's not an unreasonable goal. That's possible. The United States is in no immediate danger of imperial overstretch, although that is supposed to befall every great power in the course of time. So far, the unipolar moment looks like it's going to last for a while.

What is a threat to it is the possibility that we might make a China exception to the Bush Doctrine. In my mind, recent developments—post-Iraq, post-Afghanistan developments—inside the Bush Administration are in grave danger of creating a China exception which, in and of itself, is a huge problem. Again, I earlier said that making a coherent global strategy that makes an exception of the most likely great-power challenger to the United States is especially problematic.

Taiwan—the military balance, the strategic balance, and the cost of the Taiwan Strait—is the crucial theater or focus of this competition. It is not unlike what the Fulda Gap in Germany was to the Cold War; it is the small spot where great powers may collide. Therefore, strictly from an American strategic point of view, if we intend to preserve what you might call the *Pax Americana*, or American preeminence, the one thing above all that we must do is defend Taiwan.

Consequently, the "one China" policy is not only not sustainable, but a positive danger to our larger project of maintaining a peaceful, stable, and increasingly free world and, in particular, managing or containing the rise of China. This is something we all hope turns out as a happy story, but simply hoping that it will be true is not going to make it true. Even our struggle to transform the Middle East is a struggle against many enemies, but essentially weak enemies. What looms across the Taiwan Strait is a traditional great-power struggle.

As a final footnote, I want to say that we should also look at this with the thought that in a globalized world where China has an increasing global trade, increasing global political interests, and increasing global security interests, particularly in the Middle East, treating China as simply a regional problem is going to be perhaps self-defeating and shortsighted. The United States would not allow its energy supplies to be controlled by a hostile power or a collection of powers in the Middle East. I wonder, then, whether a growing China, an economically developing and industrializing China, an energy-importing China is likely to take a different point of view of things.

So my fundamental point is that, for the future—not simply for the future regional strategy of the United States, but for the global grand strategy of the United States—the balance across the Taiwan Strait and reversal of the "one China" policy is essential for success and the maintenance of the liberal international order that we all enjoy today.

AMBASSADOR FELDMAN: Our next speaker will be John Tkacik from The Heritage Foundation.

MR. TKACIK: I'd like to say before we start that the impetus for this conference actually came from my good friend and inspiration, Ross Terrill, who wrote this book, *The New Chinese Empire*.[10] The concept of "one China" was woven through it in such a way that it made me realize that we have to come to grips with this problem.

Who here, with the exception of the representatives from the People's Republic of China embassy, doesn't consider Taiwan to

---

[10] Ross Terrill, *The New Chinese Empire: Beijing's Political Dilemma and What It Means for the United States* (New York: Basic Books, 2003).

be a full-functioning independent country? It's a fact. We have our embassy there. We don't call it an embassy, but everybody there has e-mails at "state.gov," and the Australians at their Taipei mission receive their e-mails at "dfat.gov.au," and the Canadians are "dfait.gov.ca." The Japanese e-mails are all addressed to the Gaimusho.

Everybody considers Taiwan a country. So what is the problem? Why can't we say there are two Chinas? Or why can't we say there's "one China and one Taiwan?" The answer is that there would be a war.

This is not a philosophical problem. It's not a legal problem. It's not a moral problem. It's not an ethical problem. Instead, it's a problem of being intimidated by people that threaten war. That's it. Everybody agrees that if China said tomorrow, "Okay, we give up. We absolutely will not use force or military force to intimidate Taiwan," Taiwan would be recognized by everybody as an independent state the next day. Why? Because, frankly, it is.

For many years I have argued that America's "one China" policy is useful because it doesn't do two things. It doesn't recognize China's claims to Taiwan, and it doesn't make China angry. Never in the past century has the United States recognized Chinese sovereignty over Taiwan, and the United States has steadfastly maintained that position. This is the American position—this is the government position now, today—that China has no right in international law or otherwise to use or threaten to use force against Taiwan.

Let me begin by positing two facts.

First, by accepting and formally recognizing China's claims to territorial sovereignty over Taiwan, a country like the United States legitimates China's right to use force whenever it so wishes. Because we accept that Russia has sovereignty over Chechnya, for example, we accept that they have the right to use force in Chechnya.

Second, the less Taiwan is accepted into the international community as a fully functioning member able to make significant contributions to the general welfare, to put it bluntly, the more isolated Taiwan is in the world community and the more likely Communist China is to use force or threaten to attack democratic Taiwan.

The legal position of the United States over Taiwan, the matter of sovereignty of Taiwan, is this: Article 2 of the Japanese Peace Treaty basically says, "The sovereignty over the area is an unsettled question subject to future international resolution." An extensive history of the legal position is encompassed in a memorandum entitled "Legal Status of Taiwan," prepared by the Office of Legal Adviser in response to a request from the Director of Republic of China Affairs, dated July 13, 1971.

It is important to understand that this still remains the United States' position. On July 14, 1982, President Reagan sent a letter to Taiwan's president, Chiang Ching-kuo, which reassured him that the legal position of the United States regarding the sovereignty over Taiwan had not changed. This troublesome fact—that the international status of the area of Taiwan and the Pescadores was an "unsettled question"—ironically was also the legal position of even the exiled government of the Republic of China based in Taipei at the time. It seemed resigned to that.

In July of 1952, Republic of China Foreign Minister Yeh Kung-chao (George Yeh) informed the ROC Legislative Yuan in Taipei that, under the terms of the San Francisco Peace Treaty, no provision had been made for the return of those islands to China.[11] He continued:

> Formosa and the Pescadores were formerly Chinese territories. As Japan has renounced her claim to Formosa and the Pescadores, only China has the right to take them over. In fact, we are controlling them now and undoubtedly, they constitute a part of our territories. However, the delicate international situation makes it that they do not belong to us. Under the present circumstances, Japan has no

---

[11] See "Legal Status of Taiwan," reproduced in Appendix C of this volume.

right to transfer Formosa and the Pescadores to us,
nor can we accept such a transfer even if she so
wishes.

Although China breathes fire at the mere thought that "the
status of Taiwan remains undetermined," that concept is the core
of America's commitment to the survival and success of democracy in Taiwan today.

I say it's at the core because of a point that Henry Kissinger made
in 1976. He had gathered together all of his top China hands in his
office and asked, "If Taiwan is recognized by us as a part of China,
then it may become irresistible to them. Our saying that we want a
peaceful solution has no force. It is Chinese territory. What are we
going to do about it?"[12] To which Arthur Hummel, who would later
be the U.S. ambassador in China, said, "Down the road, perhaps,
the only solution would be an independent Taiwan."

Kissinger responded, "Well, maybe the best solution would
just be for Taiwan to be taken over by the mainland. Then that
would solve everybody's problem." At which point William
Gleysteen interjected, "I don't think that's ever going to happen."

Those were the days when diplomats actually understood what
the "one China" policy meant. It meant that we would only recognize one government of China at a time. Secretary Kissinger realized that to recognize Taiwan as part of China would legitimate
China's threats to use force against the island. When Ambassador
Leonard Woodcock negotiated normalization with Deng Xiaoping in December of 1978, he had to assure Deng Xiaoping that
the United States would not recognize the People's Republic of
China and the Republic of China together. We would only recognize one China. Hence, America's "one China" policy.

"One China" has been a code word of U.S. foreign policy
since the 1920s, when the Western powers agreed not to dismember China into autonomous warlordies dominated by individual

---

[12] William Burr, ed., *The Kissinger Transcripts: The Top Secret Talks with Beijing and Moscow*
(New York: New Press, 1999), pp. 416–417.

colonial powers. The United States had insisted since the early 1900s on an "open door" policy. U.S. policies would preserve the territorial integrity of "one China" in order to prevent the other powers from carving it up.

This policy prevented the United States from recognizing the Japanese puppet state of Manchukuo or the World War II Chinese puppet government of Wang Ching-wei. The European powers also said they had a "one China" policy and wouldn't recognize Manchukuo or Wang Ching-wei. But that was *all* that was meant by "one China." They did not mean that, somehow, every territory that had ever been under Chinese sovereignty would some day be returned to Chinese sovereignty, like Taiwan or Mongolia or Vietnam.

With the death of Generalissimo Chiang Kai-shek's son, President Chiang Ching-kuo, in January of 1988, the government of the Republic of China, no longer having any connection to China, began to lose its legitimacy. The new president, Lee Teng-hui, immediately sought to construct a new foundation of legitimacy for the ROC by restructuring the legislative Yuan and the National Assembly into parliamentary bodies that truly represented the Taiwanese people.

The new president, however, also knew the ROC could not sustain its legitimacy if it claimed to be the sovereign authority over the Chinese mainland, much less over Outer Mongolia, because to do so meant the continuation of the Chinese civil war, and as far as he was concerned, the civil war had ended in 1949.

In November of 1993, Bill Clinton, under pressure from Beijing, "disinvited" Taiwan's President Lee Teng-hui from the Asia Pacific Economic Cooperation Forum Chief Executive Summit. That was the first such summit meeting of political leaders that APEC had ever had. The United States had initially invited President Lee Teng-hui but then disinvited him. The United States did this even though APEC's bylaws mandated that all member economies be treated equally.

It is my belief that this incident was one of the factors that impressed on President Lee Teng-hui the urgency of creating a new identity for Taiwan as separate from China.

At that summit, President Lee Teng-hui's personal representative, Chiang Ping-kun, read a statement proclaiming Taiwan's interim "two Chinas policy," which declared that "[t]he term China has
distinct geographic, historical, and cultural connotations, and within China there are two independent, sovereign, and mutually non-
subordinate nations." He said *Guojia*, and that was something that
he had written, taking notes from a meeting with President Lee
before leaving Taipei for the Seattle APEC summit.[13]

Following the collapse of the Soviet Union, China continued
to pursue a course of military modernization; this time, however,
China's military objectives were no longer focused on a Soviet
threat. They focused on Taiwan. China's military has justified vast
expenditures on advanced weaponry to deter American involvement in a Taiwan Strait crisis.

In 1995 and 1996, the U.S. repeatedly assured China that it
pursued a "one China" policy. Despite these reassurances, China
twice launched mock missile attacks in the Taiwan Strait, which
halted all civilian, maritime, and aviation traffic in the heavily
traveled sea lanes and air lanes for days. In 1995, the State Department responded to the missile strikes by saying that these did not
contribute to peace and stability in the region. Emboldened, the
next Chinese missile attacks struck closer to Taiwan's land, finally
obliging the United States to take more forceful action than merely chastising China for "actions that are not conducive to stability
in the Strait."

I'm reminded that on December 16, 2003, just two months ago,
when State Department spokesman Richard Boucher was asked
about Chinese missile deployments against Taiwan, he said, "We
have felt that missile deployments are not conducive to dialogue."

QUESTION: Last one. Taiwan's vice president
today described the Chinese missiles pointed at the

---

[13] See "Officials on Charges of 'Interim Two Chinas' Policy," broadcast on "Hookup,"
Taipei China Broadcasting Corporation News Network (in Mandarin Chinese), November 23, 1993, transcribed by Foreign Broadcast Information Service.

island as a form of "state terrorism." Do you have
any reaction to that?

MR. BOUCHER: I don't want to get into the political rhetoric that's in Taiwan or how various people
phrase things. We've always made clear that we felt
that China's ballistic missiles opposite Taiwan height-
en tensions. They have always been a factor in our
thinking as we seek to make sure that we're living up
to our obligations vis-à-vis Taiwan's legitimate defensive needs. We have felt that missile deployments are
not conducive to a dialogue. We've also supported
resolution of the issues in this region by dialogue.[14]

I think China is getting the wrong message here. I won't char-
acterize President Bush's statements in December relating to
moves by Taiwan's president to hold a referendum designed to
protest China's missile threat to his country, but I will say that
Chinese premier Wen Jiabao seems to have gotten the impression that the United States was against Taiwan independence and
consequently seemed to have the philosophical idea that, therefore, Taiwan was still a dependent territory of China.

In an article that he wrote in December shortly after that visit,
Willy Lam quoted a Politburo member as saying that, after we
deal with President Bush, the Chinese impression is:

if Chen Shui-bian were to disturb the status quo by
holding referendums and other means, and we
were to respond militarily, the U.S. cannot raise
objections, let alone interfere. After all, Bush has
already indicated unambiguous opposition to
attempts by Taiwan to change the status quo.[15]

---

[14] U.S. Department of State, "Daily Press Briefing," December 16, 2003, at *www.state.
gov/r/pa/prs/dpb/2003/27327.htm*.
[15] Willy Wo-Lap Lam, "China Claims a Big Win over Taiwan," CNN.COM, December 15,

Now let me read you what Deputy Secretary of State Richard
Armitage said in Beijing: "The fact of the matter is, it's now twenty-five years since we normalized relations."[16] This year, 2004—
25 years after normalization—Mr. Armitage added that "the question of Taiwan has been handled sensitively and sensibly" by both
governments of Beijing and Taiwan.[17]

This is what John Kerry said when he was asked about the Taiwan issue:

> [T]he United States has always had a one China
> policy, notwithstanding how terrible we may under-
> stand their regime to be. And that has been a
> Republican president, Democrat president policy
> alike. I think it is the right policy.[18]

Then he said that the way for us to resolve this issue is to tell
Taiwan that "we are not going to permit them to declare independence; that would be unacceptable."[19] Finally, he said, "I think
the way we resolve it is to continue to push, as we did with Hong
Kong, Macao and other places, for a 'one China, two systems'
[policy]."[20]

This is truly frightening. A top Republican Administration
diplomat is characterizing China's handling of Taiwan as "sensitive and sensible," and a man who could conceivably be President
this time next year says the United States should resolve the Taiwan problem by continuing to push for a "one China, two systems"

2003, at *http://edition.cnn.com/2003/WORLD/asiapcf/east/12/15/willy.column/index.html*
(December 17, 2003).

[16] Transcript of "Media Round Table, Richard L. Armitage, Deputy Secretary of State,
Beijing, China, January 30, 2004, at *www.state.gov/s/d/rm/28614.htm.*

[17] *Ibid.*

[18] See transcript, "National Public Radio Democratic Presidential Candidates Debate,"
January 6, 2004, at
www.vote-smart.org/debate_transcripts/trans_29.pdf. See also "Democrat Primaries Candidate Blasts Bush Attitude Toward Taiwan," Taipei Central News Agency, January 7, 2004.

[19] *Ibid.*

[20] *Ibid.*

formula. This is why the words "one China" have ceased to be useful, if they ever were, as a description of American policy.

"One China, two systems" is Beijing's formula, not ours. Beijing forced this formula on Hong Kong, not us. Yet there are responsible elected representatives and intelligent diplomats who have adopted China's meaning of the phrase "one China" instead of our own.

Why is that? It's because America's "one China" policy doesn't mean "one China," while China's "one China" policy does mean "one China." So, obviously, if you don't understand the policy, you assume that the phrase "one China" reflects the formula that seems to make more sense.

Let me add that I was gratified three weeks ago when my good friend and hero, Deputy Assistant Secretary of State for East Asia and Pacific Affairs Randall G. Schriver, described our "one China" policy. He was at the U.S.–China Economic and Security Review Commission on February 6, and he said that "We maintain our one-China policy...as defined by the three joint communiqués and the Taiwan Relations Act" and that the "three other elements that support this policy" include "our strong opposition to the use of force," "our non-support for Taiwan independence" (which is different from our opposition to it), and "our support for the Six Assurances."[21]

The Shanghai Communiqué, the Normalization Communiqué, the Taiwan Relations Act, and the Six Assurances all basically say, "We do not recognize the PRC's claims to sovereignty over one China." Under the 1933 Montevideo Convention, a state is defined as any state person that possesses the following qualifications, which Taiwan possesses in spades: The political existence of such a state is independent of recognition by other states, and its rights are based on the simple fact of its existence under international law.

---

[21] *Hearing on Military Modernization and Cross-Strait Balance,* U.S.–China Economic and Security Review Commission, 108th Cong., 2nd Sess., February 6, 2004, p.13, at *www.uscc.gov/hearings/2004hearings/transcripts/04_02_06.pdf.*

If you agree that there is one China and that Taiwan is part of China, then you agree that China has the right to use force and you legitimize their claim to use force. But if you want to make China's use of force less likely, then certainly the place to begin is by delegitimizing their claim to "one China" and their presumption that "Taiwan is part of China."

AMBASSADOR FELDMAN: The Montevideo Convention lists three characteristics to be a state: (1) defined territory, (2) defined population, and (3) the ability to enter into international agreements. Taiwan and associated islands are a defined territory. We all know that on that territory, there exists a specific population.

Some people have argued that Taiwan is not a state because it can't enter into international agreements. That's obviously false. It is a member of the World Trade Organization and many other international organizations. It has all the characteristics listed by the Montevideo Convention.

Now we turn to my friend Ross Terrill. Ross is at the Fairbank Center for East Asia at Harvard. He's written more books on China than I could possibly list in the time remaining. John has already held up the last one, *New Chinese Empire: Beijing's Political Dilemma and What It Means for the United States*, which, by the way, is reviewed in this issue of *The Journal*, which is edited by no less than John Tkacik.

ROSS TERRILL: In the 1970s, "one China," variously understood as has been said, was an effective tool for certain tasks. Certain nations such as the United States, Japan, Australia, and others wanted to establish a relationship with Beijing, and it served that purpose and did it in a number of contexts.

One was that there was the Soviet Union problem. The second was that we gave in on the theory of the situation in order to win on the practice of the situation. As John has said, we did not embrace "one China," but we acknowledged that the two authoritarian governments on both sides of the Taiwan Strait regarded Taiwan as a part of China. This did not adversely affect the concrete situation of Taiwan. That Taiwan and the mainland belong together was, of course, the KMT position of the time.

Now use of the formula bought some time for Taiwan. Unexpectedly, it bought time for a Taiwan that ceased to be authoritarian, and, as Arthur Waldron says, there was no "Plan B." The KMT didn't have a "Plan B" either, because it was not democratically minded at that time. The use of the formula, then, did have the negative effect that it missed an opportunity for Taiwan to decide to be Taiwan. James Shen didn't want that, and the KMT didn't push that in the U.N. or anywhere else.

"One China" has been twisted since then, very badly twisted—a big success for Beijing diplomacy, by the way. "One China" is not just about territorial control of all sorts of places, some now in the PRC, some outside. After all, Beijing declined to take Hong Kong for quite a while. Stalin in his last years urged Mao to take Hong Kong, and Mao said no. Beijing turned down an offer to take Macau, and Mao often said he wasn't in a hurry about Taiwan.

The kind of unity Beijing's "one China" presumes is quite complicated and quite various. Even now, Beijing might hesitate to take territorial control of Taiwan because of the problem of digesting and ruling the island. The CCP has no mechanism in place for handling a democratic portion of a decentralized realm. The current difficulties with Hong Kong are a reminder of that. There may even be officials in Beijing who realize that they could not successfully digest and rule Taiwan. So it's not just about territorial control.

Is "one China" about the unity and stability of the PRC as a sovereign nation? "One United States" would be a reasonable slogan. In fact, to insist on the "American people" over the disastrous incantations about "the peoples of the United States" would certainly be very useful.

After World War II, in the nation-building period, there was a connotation of idealistic nationalism about unity and stability. Sukarno's Indonesia, for example, used these same terms. Now sometimes we back Jakarta over a national unity issue. President Kennedy turned against the Dutch and toward Jakarta over the

Dutch West Indies (Irian Jaya now). Other times, we opposed Jakarta, with the Australians taking the lead, that we would back an independent Timor. We chose policies based on the situation at the time. Through it all, there was never any kind of "one Indonesia" theology hovering over the situation.

If "one China" means China holding together as a growing concern, stable and not flying into pieces, it could well be in American interests, bearing in mind that, historically, Russia and Japan have normally benefited from China being in a mess.

"One China," as has been said by several people, is very ambiguous. And "one China," as has also been at least implied, is in today's circumstances expansionist. Ambiguous? The three great 20th century leaders of China—Sun Yat-sen, Chiang Kai-shek, and Mao Zedong—all had different definitions of the territory of China, and some of them changed their own definition over time.

At the moment, we live in a very striking period of the unity of the Chinese realm. Even parts that the Ch'ing lost, now the PRC has back. Not to speak of the astonishing fact that the PRC has all that western segment that only became part of the Chinese court after the end of the Ming and with the Ch'ing military conquest. They were no less military conquests than the British Empire or the brief Japanese Empire were built by military conquests.

Yet many liberal Sinologists talk about a greater China. The phrase "greater Japan" is still a curse in much of East Asia, and for many surrounding peoples, "greater China" is quite a nasty phrase. Discuss "greater China" with the Vietnamese, the Mongols, the Kazakhs, the Koreans, and the Uzbeks among others, and see how you go.

There are really three reasons why "one China" is being used for expansionism. China is the only great power that claims a lot more territories—not just a few, a lot more. It's the only one that thinks like an empire. And it's the only one, one-half of whose territory—at least whose existing PRC territory—was historically lived upon by non-Han peoples. Put that into the picture when you weigh "one China" as a continuing policy of Beijing.

The gist of the matter is that "one China" is an update of an ancient technique of Chinese imperial statecraft. It was called all sorts of other names—basically "all under heaven," or variations of "all under heaven," *tian xia.* "All under heaven" meant the realm of the Chinese court. Then there were other phrases—*tian xia wei gong,* "public good everywhere under heaven," and so on. So, in the broader sense, we're dealing still with the last stages of a shift from a universal kingship, or what I call "civilizational rule," to "modern state rule." Some of John's penetrating points about realism are really to say that the world of the nation-state and its values are not being applied to this situation.

For two thousand years, predecessor notions of "one China" were an ideal and tools for contenders of power to establish legitimacy to deal with enemies and rivals. Doesn't that ring a bit of a bell in recent history? It wasn't limited to China. Vietnam, Korea, Tibet—they were all subject to this world-arranging, self-given task of the Chinese court. A few weeks ago, none other than Nguyen Cao Ky, the former prime minister in Saigon, visited Hanoi. He was very impressed with the Chinese economy, and he said that "economically China could destroy Vietnam and the government"—meaning the Hanoi government—"knows it." Then he added, "Vietnam could become a district of China again."[22]

In the ancient classic, *The Book of Rights,* we find the phrase, "There can be no two suns under heaven." Since there was no distinction between Chinese civilization and civilization, this was, if you like, a "one world" doctrine. But the unity was sometimes there and sometimes not there, and fictions had to be evolved to explain its absence. Sometimes a terrible absence, as when non-Chinese people took over the whole Chinese system.

Quite beyond the Taiwan issue, "one China" today helps Beijing, which has grafted Leninism onto elements of a Chinese autocratic tradition to exaggerate the longevity of Chinese identity.

---

[22] See New York Times News Service, "At US urging, Former South Vietnamese Official Visits Home City After 50 Years," *Taipei Times,* January 27, 2004, p. 5, at *www.taipeitimes.com/News/world/archives/2004/01/27/2003092629.*

This is all part of the propaganda of the "one China" doctrine: to exaggerate the cohesion of Chinese civilization and to shore up the legitimacy of the PRC regime.

I criticized the KMT at the start. In Chiang Kai-shek's book, *China's Destiny*, we find the phrase, "without the Kuomintang today there would be no China."[23] The idea of China conflated with the idea of a unified state under a certain party's rule—both Mao and Chiang Kai-shek were heirs to that, which makes us realize how far things have changed, as John and others said, when they're essentially trying to bring light onto the situation by saying, "we live in a world of nation states and we live a post-9/11 world as well." Of course, it's a concept that doesn't suit Chen Shui-bian, Martin Lee, the Dalai Lama, the government of Mongolia, and a long list of others because they are not heir to this thinking behind it.

For American policy, there's good news and bad news about "one China" as being built on Chinese statecraft. The nature of the unity fluctuated. It was never the unity of, say, the British Empire— courts, flags, schools, "God save the King," and all that—and there were many periods when China's grip was very, very loose.

To sum it up, there was an arrogance of spirit. Listen to Mao not long before he died:

> About a hundred years ago, the area to the east of Lake Baikal became Russian territory. And since then Vladivostok and Kamchatka in other areas have become Soviet territory. We have not yet presented our account for this list.[24]

He repeated those words to Henry Kissinger in 1973, except that he'd added a bit of extra territory. And yet, the arrogance was sometimes married to a policy passivity. Maybe tomorrow, as Tom perhaps is foreshadowing, China will want that part of Siberia. But any reaching by China for this can be deterred.

---

[23] Chiang Kai-shek, *China's Destiny* (New York, Roy Publishers, 1947), p. 222.
[24] Burr, ed., *The Kissinger Transcripts*, p. 187.

So the mixed picture is this: It's highly unusual for a modern nation-state to guard the huge list of residual claims, demands, aspirations, and weird doctrines like "one China" that Beijing does. On the other hand, China is in some ways a normal nation-state. It backs down. It counts the numbers. It can be destroyed—it can be deterred. There's a lot of evidence, I suggest, for that.

Reunification of Taiwan with the mainland is an issue that's pretty much passed by. Taiwan's been independent for half a century and out of China's control for the half-century before that. The time and opportunity was when the government of Taiwan agreed with Beijing that Taiwan was part of China. No government in Taiwan today is going to fuss over formal words in such a way as to endanger the people of Taiwan. They're on the front line, not us.

There would have to be some blend of at least two of three factors to give Beijing a last-ditch chance. America would have to turn its back, the Taiwan elites would have to lose the will to run their own show, and the Chinese army would have to have a moment of freedom and incentive to take a risk. At least two of those things would have to obtain. I see it all receding.

The whole issue is now an Asia–Pacific balance-of-power issue. Tom has covered that well. Sometimes our allies get a bit frustrated that America seems to think the Taiwan issue is its issue. Japan, Australia, the Philippines, Vietnam—the list is long—would all be enormously affected by the incorporation of Taiwan into the PRC.

Beijing itself has high priorities that conflict with it. If you were Hu Jintao today, and you had to chose between accepting the established independence of Taiwan today with all that would be involved in overthrowing that or keeping a situation where 30 percent of your exports go to the United States, which would you chose?

Beijing has to decide whether to keep up with the anti-hegemony, anti-imperialist framework of its rhetoric, because that's what the Taiwan project is about. Taiwan was a colony of Japan. The Cairo Declaration in 1943 said "it all goes back." But American power and globalization have become inextricable. So a China in the WTO is a China enmeshed with capitalism in the U.S. and elsewhere.

How can you be anti-imperialist if you wish to participate in the globalization that the imperialists spearhead? China is not an aggrieved former semi-colony, struggling to emerge from victim status and get extra territories. It's a would-be expansionist power whose current leadership hopes to eclipse the U.S. as a leading force in Asia.

If those two points are correct, I think we should be "formally agnostic about Taiwan's status" (in the phrase of the 1971 State Department); and within that formal agnosticism, we should lean to independence for Taiwan in the same way that Bill Clinton leaned toward reunification, by putting it seemingly on the agenda. One day, we may be able to acknowledge the independence of Taiwan. For the moment, a position of agnosticism where we say, "it's not ultimately the United States' business for the moment," but preserving the deterrence and leaning toward increasing *de facto* acknowledgement of independence, is the right choice.

AMBASSADOR FELDMAN: Just to sum up a very complicated discussion, I emphasize once again: It is not United States policy to recognize, assert, or agree that Taiwan is a part of the People's Republic of China. Similarly, it is not United States policy to recognize any government of China other than the government in Beijing.

That being the case, one would have to think about what would be the policy consequences if we were to say that there is a government in China, and there is a government in Taiwan, and they are different. Supposing we were to agree with Chen Shui-bian's *Yibian Yiguo* (one country on each side of the Taiwan Strait), we would have to think about what the consequences of that would be.

Questions are now open. Shirley?

SHIRLEY KAN: I am Shirley Kan with the Library of Congress's Congressional Research Service. You had a number of quotes up there, John, but we also know that part of the record, to be comprehensive, is that we had a Republican President, President Nixon, who said, "there is one China and Taiwan is a part of China."

We also have a current Republican President who has now said over and over privately that we are against or opposed to Taiwan independence. He has stood next to Hu Jintao or Wen Jiabao three times now when these leaders have said that "Bush said we oppose Taiwan independence," and Bush neither contradicted them nor corrected them.

It's hard to imagine a situation where, under either a Republican or Democratic President, you can achieve the goals that you have set out. So I would like to ask how you would fashion a realistic strategy for what you're advocating.

AMBASSADOR FELDMAN: Before I turn this over to John to answer, let me just say that privately conveyed remarks by any American leader, including a President of the United States, cannot constitute a binding obligation of the United States government. Such obligations can be construed only within formal international documents and not by private statements. If Henry Kissinger said to Zhou Enlai, "I think it's great that you take Taiwan," that doesn't make it American policy.

MR. TKACIK: In the Normalization Communiqué, it says the United States acknowledges the Chinese position that there's "one China and that Taiwan is part of China." Then Warren Christopher goes to the Congress and says the United States has not itself agreed to this position.

Everybody that has read the negotiating record knows that there was a big discussion about this issue of *chengren* or *renshidao* as part of the Normalization Communiqué: whether "acknowledge" means to "recognize in the formal diplomatic way" (*chengren*) or "just take note of" (*renshidao*). And the United States basically said, "You translate it the way you want to translate it, but we'll translate it the way we want to translate it, and this is our translation: The United States has not agreed to this position."

That was our view. The Taiwan Relations Act, which is the law of the land, basically says that whenever U.S. law refers to foreign countries, nation-states, or governments, those laws apply to Taiwan. The way you would say it is: From now on, the American policy is as we have always said it. It is based on the "Three Communiqués," the Taiwan Relations Act, and, as Secretary Schriver added, the "Six Assurances." Basically, let the Chinese know that we do not accept their claim to sovereignty and we do not accept the legitimacy of their threats.

MS. KAN: John, I don't mean to parse the last 33 years of the record. My question was about what is the strategy? As Tom Donnelly rightly emphasized, we're talking about strategy here.

AMBASSADOR FELDMAN: Arthur, do you want to do that?

DR. WALDRON: I think it is important, actually, to get the record straight. I remember very well in the Clinton Administration Assistant Secretary for East Asia Winston Lord, who allegedly had the China account. I asked him, "Have you seen every document that the U.S. and the PRC have exchanged?" And he said, "Absolutely not. I have no idea what's been said."

That's the typical example of how badly prepared we Americans are, and also of the fact that China policy is always made in secret. This recent thing with Wen Jiabao and so forth—the State Department was cut out of it; the Department of Defense was cut out of it.

It's important to remember that when policy is made in secret, by whispers, by Kissinger disappearing on a plane for Rawalpindi and so forth, that policy does not have the same kind of robustness that policy has if it's made in the light of day with consultation. It's a peculiarity of China policy that it's always done in this kind of conspiratorial way, and that renders it very weak. It also suggests that it doesn't have much support.

If you look at Nixon's last book, he said that, in fact, Taiwan and China are going to remain separate politically—he writes that quite explicitly—but that they are intertwined economically. So I think it's quite wrong to say that Nixon endorsed the idea that Taiwan was part of China.

As to how we proceed now, we're in a rather difficult position, as I stated. We've dug ourselves rather deeply into a hole. It's as if you miss a turn on a turnpike or you're going to Dulles Airport or something; you turn the wrong way, and then you discover you have to drive to Newark before you have a chance to correct it.

We have thrown away so many opportunities. We have missed so many chances. We have said so many things that we shouldn't say, that turning this thing around is going to be very difficult. However, it's going to be essential. It isn't going to just happen. This is a sort of a 1970s perception of what the world was like. The world has changed tremendously, and it's never going to go back to the way it was then. Therefore, we have to find tools to deal with this reality.

Normally, when you deal with a nation-state, you have ambassadors. The head of state can come to the White House. If you really want to schmooze him, you take him up to the private headquarters and so forth. These are the essential tools of diplomacy.

In dealing with Taiwan—which, if you were to list our national security concerns, is certainly in the top ten; for Japan, it's in the top five—we have discarded all of these tools. This was a very foolish thing to do.

You say, "who destabilized the situation?" *Now* we're worried about stabilization. In 1979, if we'd done a better negotiating job and we hadn't assumed that Taiwan was going to disappear, but we'd rather made some sort of provision—and we could easily have gotten that if we had insisted on it—we wouldn't have an unstable situation there because everything would be well defined. But we were scripting. So now we say Chen Shui-bian is destabilizing things.

Actually, the United States is the one that destabilized the situation, and as I said before, the way that you fix this is first to stop talking "make-believe." Let's stop playing make-believe. Let's stop engaging in all of these rituals of where can the ROC representatives meet people. A Taiwan diplomat has called Washington the *Zijin Cheng*—the Forbidden City—because their president can go to the Waldorf Astoria but he can't come to Washington.

This is just nonsense, and we've got to begin to discard it and to explain to China why we're doing it; explain why it's in their interest that this not become a bone of contention; and, as Ross pointed out very well, realize that a lot of other countries have stakes. This is not simply an American issue.

There's a very interesting analysis from the International Crisis Group, which is in Brussels. They say that if China invaded Taiwan, you would almost certainly get recognition of an independent Taiwan, not just by the United States, but by the European Union—even if Taiwan were occupied. During the period of this occupation, there would be great repression, and the result would be, essentially, the complete exclusion of China from world markets. And that would mean massive unemployment in coastal China and disorder.

I think it's very, very important that China understand this, because I think sometimes they kid themselves and they think that they can finesse it.

AMBASSADOR FELDMAN: I just want to point out that I do believe that when President Bush says he opposes independence for Taiwan, it's that he misread the briefing book. The policy is so recondite that you're supposed to say, "We do not support independence for Taiwan." It's very easy for somebody to read that and say, "We oppose independence for Taiwan." What it comes down to is, should we have a policy that is so artificial and so recondite that the normal intelligent person really cannot understand it? Tom?

MR. DONNELLY: The important number is the two aircraft carriers during the 1995 and '96 missile embargo crisis. When stuff really starts to happen, all this diplomatic stuff gets set aside because the crisis immediately becomes an American crisis and a crisis for America's allies in the region. It's not simply a China–Taiwan issue. Even the Clinton Administration was compelled to take serious military steps to try to make sure that the crisis didn't actually come to a shooting war. And to me, if Bill Clinton will do it, then any President will do it.

MR. TERRILL: I don't think the situation's quite as bleak as you said, Arthur. The make-believe has worked. Lee Teng-hui and

Chen Shui-bian have done an awful lot toward making Taiwan fully independent by just slicing pieces of salami off one by one. This has been a historic change that's been done by smoke and mirrors. So sometimes it can help.

On the U.S. end, let's distinguish between the physical status quo and the political status quo. I think President Bush has done a good job in saying America is strong to defend the physical status quo—whatever it takes: the word "obligation," as Tom said, more arms. And he has talked a lot about democracy, which is another way of saying that, since our policy is "we don't support a change without the will of the people involved," the PRC has got to be democratic, too, before we could support it. He's been quite strong.

Where the remark with Wen Jiabao was unfortunate is that you can't freeze the political status quo. We want to freeze the physical status quo in the Taiwan Strait, but you cannot stop the evolution of Chinese politics. Above all, you should not have to be in a position either of saying their referendums are wrong or, as the Congressman said this morning, passing votes saying their referendums are fine. We should just be able to keep our hands off the whole thing and stick to the territorial status quo, not talk about the political status quo.

AMBASSADOR FELDMAN: Last question goes to Ms. Shaheen.[25]

THERESE SHAHEEN: I feel compelled to defend the United States government. While it's made up of human beings who are all frail—and we're all frail—I think Ross really has it 99.9 percent correct.

I want to make a point here, lest I wrong your Chinese audience. President Bush did not say the word "referendum" in his remark. He said "no unilateral change in the status quo." This idea that he has talked about a referendum is a fiction as far as I know. He talked about "no unilateral change in the status quo." As Ross said, the salami keeps getting cut.

What is the status quo? Well, the status quo is what you've all described here. So I'm not sure that President Bush has got it wrong. I think he's got it right, and that's why I think what he said was very carefully worded. I think some of what he said was manipulated by other parties, but what he said was right on the money.

MR. DONNELLY: I think technically you're right, but I'm worried that in the larger sense, there's something else going on here. I am very worried that there's an attempt to substitute the global war on terrorism for the Cold War strategic rationale that gave life to this dilemma in the first place.

I think the "one China" policy is headed for the dustbin of history, and the guys who are trying to breathe life into it, to keep it going, are, as John has written very persuasively, exploiting the war on terrorism. They tried to construct a larger strategic framework for preserving the normal status quo relationship with Beijing, and what I think is going on is an attempt to shape the Bush Doctrine to preserve a China exception to it, and I worry very deeply about that even though you can parse any particular event or any particular presidential or bureaucratic statement to convince yourself that something else is going on.

AMBASSADOR FELDMAN: "Status quo" is such a wonderful phrase. We say we want to preserve the status quo. We want to go back to the status quo. That would mean it's not the status quo. Last word. John?

MR. TKACIK: I wrote an article in 2002 called "Don't Change 'One China' Policy, Explain It."[26] What I was trying to get to was that we already have a policy that works; it's just that we're too afraid to talk about it. When Randy Schriver mentioned the Six

---

[26]John Tkacik, "Don't Change 'One China' Policy, Explain It," *Taiwan News* (Taipei), September 5, 2002, p. 8, at *www.etaiwannews.com/Opinion/2002/09/05/1021559598.htm*

Assurances, one of which is "The United States has not altered its position regarding sovereignty over Taiwan," why don't we say that? Why not come out and say, "We don't take a position on the status quo"?

AMBASSADOR FELDMAN: There's one that's even more important: "The United States will not play any mediation role between Taiwan and Beijing." That should be engraved in letters of gold and given to every Administration.

This is a problem for the two sides to solve. Our policy should be "We can accept whatever solution the two sides come up with as long as it is not the result of military coercion and as long as it has the absolute, irrevocable consent of the people of Taiwan."

Appendix B

Taiwan Relations Act

United States Code, Title 22,
Chapter 48, Sections 3301–3316
Enacted April 10, 1979

[Editor's Note: Several revisions were made to Public Law 96–8 when it was codified. Sections 1 and 18 were omitted, as was Section 12(d). In addition, the United States Code contains a section not included in the original Act, Section 3310a. The United States Code version is the authoritative version of the Act.]

- § 3301. Congressional findings and declaration of policy.
  - (a) Findings.
  - (b) Policy.
  - (c) Human rights.
- § 3302. Implementation of United States policy with regard to Taiwan.
  - (a) Defense articles and services.
  - (b) Determination of Taiwan's defense needs.
  - (c) United States response to threats to Taiwan or dangers to United States interests.
- § 3303. Application to Taiwan of laws and international agreements.
  - (a) Application of United States laws generally.
  - (b) Application of United States laws in specific and enumerated areas.
  - (c) Treaties and other international agreements.
  - (d) Membership in international financial institutions and other international organizations.
- § 3303. Overseas Private Investment Corporation.
  - (a) Removal of per capita income restriction on Corporation activities with respect to investment projects on Taiwan.
  - (b) Application by Corporation of other criteria.
- § 3305. The American Institute in Taiwan.
  - (a) Conduct of programs, transactions, or other relations with respect to Taiwan.

- ○ (b) Agreements or transactions relative to Taiwan entered into, performed, and enforced.
- ○ (c) Preemption of laws, rules, regulations, or ordinances of District of Columbia, States, or political subdivisions of States.
- § 3306. Services to United States citizens on Taiwan.
  - ○ (a) Authorized services.
  - ○ (b) Acts by authorized employees.
- § 3307. Exemption from taxation.
  - ○ (a) United States, State, or local taxes.
  - ○ (b) Charitable contributions; transfers for public, charitable, and religious uses; charitable and similar gifts.
- § 3308. Activities of United States Government agencies.
  - ○ (a) Sale, loans, or lease of property; administrative and technical support functions and services.
  - ○ (b) Acquisition and acceptance of services.
  - ○ (c) Institute books and records; access; audit.
- § 3309. Taiwan instrumentality.
  - ○ (a) Establishment of instrumentality; Presidential determination of necessary authority.
  - ○ (b) Offices and personnel.
  - ○ (c) Privileges and immunities.
- § 3310. Employment of United States Government agency personnel.
  - ○ (a) Separation from Government service; reemployment or reinstatement upon termination of Institute employment; benefits.
  - ○ (b) Employment of aliens on Taiwan.
  - ○ (c) Institute employees not deemed United States employees.
  - ○ (d) Tax treatment of amounts paid Institute employees.
- § 3310a. Commercial personnel at American Institute of Taiwan.
- § 3311. Reporting requirements.
  - ○ (a) Texts of agreements to be transmitted to Congress; secret agreements to be transmitted to Senate Foreign Relations Committee and House Foreign Affairs Committee.
  - ○ (b) Agreements.
  - ○ (c) Congressional notification, review, and approval requirements and procedures.
- § 3312. Rules and regulations.
- § 3313. Congressional oversight.
  - ○ (a) Monitoring activities of Senate Foreign Relations Committee, House Foreign Affairs Committee, and other Congressional committees.
  - ○ (b) Committee reports to their respective Houses.
- § 3314. Definitions.
- § 3315. Authorization of appropriations.
- § 3316. Severability.

United States Code
TITLE 22—FOREIGN RELATIONS AND INTERCOURSE
CHAPTER 48—TAIWAN RELATIONS

- **Sec. 3301. Congressional findings and declaration of policy**
  - (a) Findings

  The President having terminated governmental relations between the United States and the governing authorities on Taiwan recognized by the United States as the Republic of China prior to January 1, 1979, the Congress finds that the enactment of this chapter is necessary—
    - (1) to help maintain peace, security, and stability in the Western Pacific; and
    - (2) to promote the foreign policy of the United States by authorizing the continuation of commercial, cultural, and other relations between the people of the United States and the people on Taiwan.
  - (b) Policy

  It is the policy of the United States—
    - (1) to preserve and promote extensive, close, and friendly commercial, cultural, and other relations between the people of the United States and the people on Taiwan, as well as the people on the China mainland and all other peoples of the Western Pacific area;
    - (2) to declare that peace and stability in the area are in the political, security, and economic interests of the United States, and are matters of international concern;
    - (3) to make clear that the United States decision to establish diplomatic relations with the People's Republic of China rests upon the expectation that the future of Taiwan will be determined by peaceful means;
    - (4) to consider any effort to determine the future of Taiwan by other than peaceful means, including by boycotts or embargoes, a threat to the peace and security of the Western Pacific area and of grave concern to the United States;
    - (5) to provide Taiwan with arms of a defensive character; and
    - (6) to maintain the capacity of the United States to resist any resort to force or other forms of coercion that would jeopardize the security, or the social or economic system, of the people on Taiwan.
  - (c) Human rights

  Nothing contained in this chapter shall contravene the interest of the United States in human rights, especially with respect to the human rights of all the approximately eighteen million inhabitants of Taiwan. The preservation and enhancement of the human rights of all the people on Taiwan are hereby reaffirmed as objectives of the United States.

- **Sec. 3302. Implementation of United States policy with regard to Taiwan**
  - (a) Defense articles and services
    In furtherance of the policy set forth in section 3301 of this title, the United States will make available to Taiwan such defense articles and defense services in such quantity as may be necessary to enable Taiwan to maintain a sufficient self-defense capability.
  - (b) Determination of Taiwan's defense needs
    The President and the Congress shall determine the nature and quantity of such defense articles and services based solely upon their judgment of the needs of Taiwan, in accordance with procedures established by law. Such determination of Taiwan's defense needs shall include review by United States military authorities in connection with recommendations to the President and the Congress.
  - (c) United States response to threats to Taiwan or dangers to United States interests
    The President is directed to inform the Congress promptly of any threat to the security or the social or economic system of the people on Taiwan and any danger to the interests of the United States arising therefrom. The President and the Congress shall determine, in accordance with constitutional processes, appropriate action by the United States in response to any such danger.

- **Sec. 3303. Application to Taiwan of laws and international agreements**
  - (a) Application of United States laws generally
    The absence of diplomatic relations or recognition shall not affect the application of the laws of the United States with respect to Taiwan, and the laws of the United States shall apply with respect to Taiwan in the manner that the laws of the United States applied with respect to Taiwan prior to January 1, 1979.
  - (b) Application of United States laws in specific and enumerated areas
    The application of subsection (a) of this section shall include, but shall not be limited to, the following:
    - (1) Whenever the laws of the United States refer or relate to foreign countries, nations, states, governments, or similar entities, such terms shall include and such laws shall apply with respect to Taiwan.
    - (2) Whenever authorized by or pursuant to the laws of the United States to conduct or carry out programs, transactions, or other relations with respect to foreign countries, nations, states, governments, or similar entities, the President or any agency of the United States Government is authorized to conduct and carry out, in accordance with section 3305 of this title, such programs, transactions, and other relations with respect to Taiwan (including, but not limited to, the performance of services for the United States through contracts with commercial entities on Taiwan), in accordance with the applicable laws of the United States.
    - (3)
    - (A) The absence of diplomatic relations and recognition with respect to Taiwan shall not abrogate, infringe, modify, deny, or

otherwise affect in any way any rights or obligations (including but not limited to those involving contracts, debts, or property interests of any kind) under the laws of the United States heretofore or hereafter acquired by or with respect to Taiwan.

- (B) For all purposes under the laws of the United States, including actions in any court in the United States, recognition of the People's Republic of China shall not affect in any way the ownership of or other rights or interests in properties, tangible and intangible, and other things of value, owned or held on or prior to December 31, 1978, or thereafter acquired or earned by the governing authorities on Taiwan.
- (4) Whenever the application of the laws of the United States depends upon the law that is or was applicable on Taiwan or compliance therewith, the law applied by the people on Taiwan shall be considered the applicable law for that purpose.
- (5) Nothing in this chapter, nor the facts of the President's action in extending diplomatic recognition to the People's Republic of China, the absence of diplomatic relations between the people on Taiwan and the United States, or the lack of recognition by the United States, and attendant circumstances thereto, shall be construed in any administrative or judicial proceeding as a basis for any United States Government agency, commission, or department to make a finding of fact or determination of law, under the Atomic Energy Act of 1954 (42 U.S.C. 2011 et seq.) and the Nuclear Non-Proliferation Act of 1978 (22 U.S.C. 3201 et seq.), to deny an export license application or to revoke an existing export license for nuclear exports to Taiwan.
- (6) For purposes of the Immigration and Nationality Act (8 U.S.C. 1101 et seq.), Taiwan may be treated in the manner specified in the first sentence of section 202(b) of that Act (8 U.S.C. 1152(b)).
- (7) The capacity of Taiwan to sue and be sued in courts in the United States, in accordance with the laws of the United States, shall not be abrogated, infringed, modified, denied, or otherwise affected in any way by the absence of diplomatic relations or recognition.
- (8) No requirement, whether expressed or implied, under the laws of the United States with respect to maintenance of diplomatic relations or recognition shall be applicable with respect to Taiwan.
- (c) Treaties and other international agreements
  For all purposes, including actions in any court in the United States, the Congress approves the continuation in force of all treaties and other international agreements, including multilateral conventions, entered into by the United States and the governing authorities on Taiwan recognized by the United States as the Republic of China prior to January 1, 1979, and in force between them on December 31, 1978, unless and until terminated in accordance with law.
- (d) Membership in international financial institutions and other international organizations

Nothing in this chapter may be construed as a basis for supporting the exclusion or expulsion of Taiwan from continued membership in any international financial institution or any other international organization.

- **Sec. 3304. Overseas Private Investment Corporation**
  - (a) Removal of per capita income restriction on Corporation activities with respect to investment projects on Taiwan
    During the three-year period beginning on April 10, 1979, the $1,000 per capita income restriction in clause (2) of the second undesignated paragraph of section 2191 of this title shall not restrict the activities of the Overseas Private Investment Corporation in determining whether to provide any insurance, reinsurance, loans, or guaranties with respect to investment projects on Taiwan.
  - (b) Application by Corporation of other criteria
    Except as provided in subsection (a) of this section, in issuing insurance, reinsurance, loans, or guaranties with respect to investment projects on Taiwan, the Overseas Private [Investment] Corporation shall apply the same criteria as those applicable in other parts of the world.

- **Sec. 3305. The American Institute in Taiwan**
  - (a) Conduct of programs, transactions, or other relations with respect to Taiwan
    Programs, transactions, and other relations conducted or carried out by the President or any agency of the United States Government with respect to Taiwan shall, in the manner and to the extent directed by the President, be conducted and carried out by or through—
    - (1) The American Institute in Taiwan, a nonprofit corporation incorporated under the laws of the District of Columbia, or
    - (2) such comparable successor nongovernmental entity as the President may designate, (hereafter in this chapter referred to as the "Institute").
  - (b) Agreements or transactions relative to Taiwan entered into, performed, and enforced
    Whenever the President or any agency of the United States Government is authorized or required by or pursuant to the laws of the United States to enter into, perform, enforce, or have in force an agreement or transaction relative to Taiwan, such agreement or transaction shall be entered into, performed, and enforced, in the manner and to the extent directed by the President, by or through the Institute.
  - (c) Preemption of laws, rules, regulations, or ordinances of District of Columbia, States, or political subdivisions of States
    To the extent that any law, rule, regulation, or ordinance of the District of Columbia, or of any State or political subdivision thereof in which the Institute is incorporated or doing business, impedes or otherwise interferes with the performance of the functions of the Institute pursuant to this chapter, such law, rule, regulation, or ordinance shall be deemed to be preempted by this chapter.

- **Sec. 3306. Services to United States citizens on Taiwan**
  - (a) Authorized services
    The Institute may authorize any of its employees on Taiwan—
    - (1) to administer to or take from any person an oath, affirmation, affidavit, or deposition, and to perform any notarial act which any notary public is required or authorized by law to perform within the United States;
    - (2) [t]o act as provisional conservator of the personal estates of deceased United States citizens; and
    - (3) to assist and protect the interests of United States persons by performing other acts such as are authorized to be performed outside the United States for consular purposes by such laws of the United States as the President may specify.
  - (b) Acts by authorized employees
    Acts performed by authorized employees of the Institute under this section shall be valid, and of like force and effect within the United States, as if performed by any other person authorized under the laws of the United States to perform such acts.

- **Sec. 3307. Exemption from taxation**
  - (a) United States, State, or local taxes
    The Institute, its property, and its income are exempt from all taxation now or hereafter imposed by the United States (except to the extent that section 3310(a)(3) of this title requires the imposition of taxes imposed under chapter 21 of title 26, relating to the Federal Insurance Contributions Act) or by any State or local taxing authority of the United States.
  - (b) Charitable contributions; transfers for public, charitable, and religious uses; charitable and similar gifts
    For purposes of title 26, the Institute shall be treated as an organization described in sections 170(b)(1)(A), 170(c), 2055(a), 2106(a)(2)(A), 2522(a), and 2522(b) of title 26.

- **Sec. 3308. Activities of United States Government agencies**
  - (a) Sale, loans, or lease of property; administrative and technical support functions and services
    Any agency of the United States Government is authorized to sell, loan, or lease property (including interests therein) to, and to perform administrative and technical support functions and services for the operations of, the Institute upon such terms and conditions as the President may direct. Reimbursements to agencies under this subsection shall be credited to the current applicable appropriation of the agency concerned.
  - (b) Acquisition and acceptance of services
    Any agency of the United States Government is authorized to acquire and accept services from the Institute upon such terms and conditions as the President may direct. Whenever the President determines it to be in furtherance of the purposes of this chapter, the procurement of services by such agencies from the Institute may be effected without

regard to such laws of the United States normally applicable to the acquisition of services by such agencies as the President may specify by Executive order.

- ○ (c) Institute books and records; access; audit
  Any agency of the United States Government making funds available to the Institute in accordance with this chapter shall make arrangements with the Institute for the Comptroller General of the United States to have access to the books and records of the Institute and the opportunity to audit the operations of the Institute.

- **Sec. 3309. Taiwan instrumentality**
  - ○ (a) Establishment of instrumentality; Presidential determination of necessary authority
    Whenever the President or any agency of the United States Government is authorized or required by or pursuant to the laws of the United States to render or provide to or to receive or accept from Taiwan, any performance, communication, assurance, undertaking, or other action, such action shall, in the manner and to the extent directed by the President, be rendered or provided to, or received or accepted from, an instrumentality established by Taiwan which the President determines has the necessary authority under the laws applied by the people on Taiwan to provide assurances and take other actions on behalf of Taiwan in accordance with this chapter.
  - ○ (b) Offices and personnel
    The President is requested to extend to the instrumentality established by Taiwan the same number of offices and complement of personnel as were previously operated in the United States by the governing authorities on Taiwan recognized as the Republic of China prior to January 1, 1979.
  - ○ (c) Privileges and immunities
    Upon the granting by Taiwan of comparable privileges and immunities with respect to the Institute and its appropriate personnel, the President is authorized to extend with respect to the Taiwan instrumentality and its appropriate personnel, such privileges and immunities (subject to appropriate conditions and obligations) as may be necessary for the effective performance of their functions.

- **Sec. 3310. Employment of United States Government agency personnel**
  - ○ (a) Separation from Government service; reemployment or reinstatement upon termination of Institute employment; benefits
    - ■ (1) Under such terms and conditions as the President may direct, any agency of the United States Government may separate from Government service for a specified period any officer or employee of that agency who accepts employment with the Institute.
    - ■ (2) An officer or employee separated by an agency under paragraph (1) of this subsection for employment with the Institute shall be entitled upon termination of such employment to reemployment or reinstatement with such agency (or a successor agency) in an appropriate position with the attendant rights,

privileges, and benefits [which] the officer or employee would have had or acquired had he or she not been so separated, subject to such time period and other conditions as the President may prescribe.

- (3) An officer or employee entitled to reemployment or reinstatement rights under paragraph (2) of this subsection shall, while continuously employed by the Institute with no break in continuity of service, continue to participate in any benefit program in which such officer or employee was participating prior to employment by the Institute, including programs for compensation for job-related death, injury, or illness; programs for health and life insurance; programs for annual, sick, and other statutory leave; and programs for retirement under any system established by the laws of the United States; except that employment with the Institute shall be the basis for participation in such programs only to the extent that employee deductions and employer contributions, as required, in payment for such participation for the period of employment with the Institute, are currently deposited in the program's or system's fund or depository. Death or retirement of any such officer or employee during approved service with the Institute and prior to reemployment or reinstatement shall be considered a death in or retirement from Government service for purposes of any employee or survivor benefits acquired by reason of service with an agency of the United States Government.
- (4) Any officer or employee of an agency of the United States Government who entered into service with the Institute on approved leave of absence without pay prior to April 10, 1979, shall receive the benefits of this section for the period of such service.

○ (b) Employment of aliens on Taiwan
Any agency of the United States Government employing alien personnel on Taiwan may transfer such personnel, with accrued allowances, benefits, and rights, to the Institute without a break in service for purposes of retirement and other benefits, including continued participation in any system established by the laws of the United States for the retirement of employees in which the alien was participating prior to the transfer to the Institute, except that employment with the Institute shall be creditable for retirement purposes only to the extent that employee deductions and employer contributions, as required, in payment for such participation for the period of employment with the Institute, are currently deposited in the system's fund or depository.

○ (c) Institute employees not deemed United States employees
Employees of the Institute shall not be employees of the United States and, in representing the Institute, shall be exempt from section of title 18.

○ (d) Tax treatment of amounts paid Institute employees
- (1) For purposes of sections and 913 of title 26, amounts paid by the Institute to its employees shall not be treated as earned income. Amounts received by employees of the Institute shall

not be included in gross income, and shall be exempt from taxation, to the extent that they are equivalent to amounts received by civilian officers and employees of the Government of the United States as allowances and benefits which are exempt from taxation under section 912 of title 26.

- ▪ (2) Except to the extent required by subsection (a)(3) of this section, service performed in the employ of the Institute shall not constitute employment for purposes of chapter 21 of title 26 and title II of the Social Security Act (42 U.S.C. 401 et seq.).

- **Sec. 3310a. Commercial personnel at American Institute of Taiwan**

The American Institute of Taiwan shall employ personnel to perform duties similar to those performed by personnel of the United States and Foreign Commercial Service. The number of individuals employed shall be commensurate with the number of United States personnel of the Commercial Service who are permanently assigned to the United States diplomatic mission to South Korea.

- **Sec. 3311. Reporting requirements**
  - ○ (a) Texts of agreements to be transmitted to Congress; secret agreements to be transmitted to Senate Foreign Relations Committee and House Foreign Affairs Committee

    The Secretary of State shall transmit to the Congress the text of any agreement to which the Institute is a party. However, any such agreement the immediate public disclosure of which would, in the opinion of the President, be prejudicial to the national security of the United States shall not be so transmitted to the Congress but shall be transmitted to the Committee on Foreign Relations of the Senate and the Committee on Foreign Affairs of the House of Representatives under an appropriate injunction of secrecy to be removed only upon due notice from the President.
  - ○ (b) Agreements

    For purposes of subsection (a) of this section, the term "agreement" includes—

    - ▪ (1) any agreement entered into between the Institute and the governing authorities on Taiwan or the instrumentality established by Taiwan; and
    - ▪ (2) any agreement entered into between the Institute and an agency of the United States Government.
  - ○ (c) Congressional notification, review, and approval requirements and procedures

    Agreements and transactions made or to be made by or through the Institute shall be subject to the same congressional notification, review, and approval requirements and procedures as if such agreements and transactions were made by or through the agency of the United States Government on behalf of which the Institute is acting.

- **Sec. 3312. Rules and regulations**

The President is authorized to prescribe such rules and regulations as he may deem appropriate to carry out the purposes of this chapter. During the three-year period beginning on January 1, 1979, such rules and regulations shall be transmitted promptly to the Speaker of the House of Representatives and to the Committee on Foreign Relations of the Senate. Such action shall not, however, relieve the Institute of the responsibilities placed upon it by this chapter.

- **Sec. 3313. Congressional oversight**
  - (a) Monitoring activities of Senate Foreign Relations Committee, House Foreign Affairs Committee, and other Congressional committees
    The Committee on Foreign Affairs of the House of Representatives, the Committee on Foreign Relations of the Senate, and other appropriate committees of the Congress shall monitor—
    - (1) the implementation of the provisions of this chapter;
    - (2) the operation and procedures of the Institute;
    - (3) the legal and technical aspects of the continuing relationship between the United States and Taiwan; and
    - (4) the implementation of the policies of the United States concerning security and cooperation in East Asia.
  - (b) Committee reports to their respective Houses
    Such committees shall report, as appropriate, to their respective Houses on the results of their monitoring.

- **Sec. 3314. Definitions**
  For purposes of this chapter—
  - (1) the term "laws of the United States" includes any statute, rule, regulation, ordinance, order, or judicial rule of decision of the United States or any political subdivision thereof; and
  - (2) the term "Taiwan" includes, as the context may require, the islands of Taiwan and the Pescadores, the people on those islands, corporations and other entities and associations created or organized under the laws applied on those islands, and the governing authorities on Taiwan recognized by the United States as the Republic of China prior to January 1, 1979, and any successor governing authorities (including political subdivisions, agencies, and instrumentalities thereof).

- **Sec. 3315. Authorization of appropriations**
  In addition to funds otherwise available to carry out the provisions of this chapter, there are authorized to be appropriated to the Secretary of State for the fiscal year 1980 such funds as may be necessary to carry out such provisions. Such funds are authorized to remain available until expended.

- **Sec. 3316. Severability**
  If any provision of this chapter or the application thereof to any person or circumstance is held invalid, the remainder of the chapter and the application of such provision to any other person or circumstance shall not be affected thereby.

Appendix C

Memorandum
July 13, 1971

To: EA/ROC – Mr. Charles T. Sylvester
From: L/EA – Robert I. Starr
Subject: Legal Status of Taiwan

You have asked for a comprehensive memorandum analyzing the question of the legal status of Taiwan in terms suitable for Congressional presentation. Attached is a paper that should serve this purpose. It is drawn mainly from the February 3, 1961 Czyzak memorandum, and contains no sensitive information or reference to classified documents.

Concurrence: L – Mr. Salans

L:L/EA:RIStarr:cdj:7/13/71 Ex. 28900

LEGAL STATUS OF TAIWAN

<u>Prior to the Korean Hostilities</u>
From the middle of the 17th century to 1895, Formosa (Taiwan) and the Pescadores (Penghu) were part of the Chinese Empire. China then ceded these islands to Japan in 1895 in the Sino–Japanese Treaty of Shimonoseki.[1]
In the Cairo Declaration of 1943, the United States, Great Britain, and China stated it to be their purpose that "all the territories that Japan has stolen from the Chinese, such as...Formosa

and the Pescadores, shall be restored to the Republic of China".[2]
These same three governments on July 26, 1945 issued the Potsdam Proclamation declaring that "the terms of the Cairo Declaration shall be carried out and Japanese sovereignty shall be limited to the islands of Honshu, Hokkaido, Kyushu, Shikoku, and
such minor islands as we determine".[3] On August 8, 1945 the
Soviet Union adhered to the Potsdam Proclamation. By an
Imperial Rescript of September 2, 1945, the Japanese Emperor
accepted the terms of the Potsdam Declaration, and in the
Instrument of Surrender signed on the same date, the Japanese
Government "and their successors" undertook to carry out the
provisions of the Declaration.[4]

Pursuant to Japanese Imperial General Headquarters General Order No. 1, issued at the direction of the Supreme Comman-
der for the Allied Powers (SCAP), Japanese commanders in Formosa surrendered to Generalissimo Chiang Kai-shek "acting on
behalf of the United States, the Republic of China, the United
Kingdom and the British Empire, and the Union of Soviet
Socialist Republics." Continuously since that time, the Government of the Republic of China has occupied and exercised
authority over Formosa and the Pescadores.

The view of the U.S. in the intermediate post-war period
was typified by a statement on April 11, 1947 of then Acting
Secretary of State Acheson, in a letter to Senator Ball, that the
transfer of sovereignty over Formosa to China "has not yet
been formalized."

After a prolonged period of civil strife the Chinese Communists succeeded in driving the Government of the Republic of
China off the Chinese mainland. On October 1, 1949 the Chinese Communists proclaimed the establishment of the People's
Republic of China. The seat of the Government of the Republic
of China was transferred to Formosa, and in early December
1949, Taipei became its provisional capital.

Shortly thereafter, President Truman, in a statement of January 5, 1950, referred to a UN General Assembly Resolution of
December 8, 1949, (Res. 291 (IV)) which called on all states to

refrain from "(a) seeking to acquire spheres of influence or to create foreign controlled regimes within the territory of China; (b) seeking to obtain special rights or privileges within the territory of China." He said:

> "A specific application of the foregoing principles is seen in the present situation with respect to Formosa...
> "The United States has no predatory designs on Formosa or on any other Chinese territory. The United States has no desire to obtain special rights or privileges or to establish military bases on Formosa at this time...the United States Government will not pursue a course which will lead to involvement in the civil conflict in China."[5]

The Korean Conflict

The outbreak of hostilities in Korea on June 25, 1950 brought to the fore the question of the status of Formosa and the Pescadores. President Truman ordered the U.S. Seventh Fleet to prevent any attack on Formosa, and as a corollary called upon the Chinese Government on Formosa to cease all operations against the mainland. In addition, he stated that "the determination of the future status of Formosa must await the restoration of security in the Pacific, a peace settlement with Japan, or consideration by the United Nations."[6]

On August 25, 1950 the United States explained its position to the United Nations Security Council in the following terms:

> "The action of the United States was expressly to be without prejudice to the future political settlement of the status of the island. The actual status of the island is that it is territory taken from Japan by the victory of the allied forces in the Pacific. Like other such territories, its legal status

cannot be fixed until there is international action
to determine its future. The Chinese Government
was asked by the allies to take the surrender of the
Japanese forces on the Island. That is the reason
the Chinese are there now."[7]

By a letter dated September 20, 1950,[8] the United States
requested that the question of Formosa be placed on the agenda of the fifth session of the UN General Assembly. In an
explanatory note of September 21, the United States, citing the
Cairo and Potsdam declarations and the Japanese surrender,
stated nevertheless:

> "Formal transfer of Formosa to China was to
> await the conclusion of peace with Japan or some
> other appropriate formal act."

That note also stated:

> ["]The Government of the United States has
> made it abundantly clear that the measures it has
> taken with respect to Formosa were without preju-
> dice to the long-term political status of Formosa,
> and the United States has no territorial ambitions
> and seeks no special position of privilege with
> respect to Formosa. The United States believes
> further that the future of Formosa and of the
> nearly eight million people inhabited there
> should be settled by peaceful means in accor-
> dance with the Charter of the United Nations."[9]

<u>Japanese Peace Treaty</u>
    From September 4 to 8, 1951 a conference for the conclusion
and signature of a Treaty of Peace with Japan was held at San Francisco. China was not represented at the Conference because of the
disagreement among the participants as to who actually represent-

ed the government of that country. Reflecting this disagreement is article 2 of the Peace Treaty, which reads in its pertinent part:

> "(b) Japan renounces all right, title and claim to Formosa and the Pescadores."[10]

John Foster Dulles, U.S. delegate at the Conference, commented on this provision in article 2:

> "Some Allied Powers suggested that article 2 should not merely delimit Japanese sovereignty according to Potsdam, but specify precisely the ultimate disposition of each of the ex-Japanese territories. This, admittedly, would have been neater. But it would have raised questions as to which there are now no agreed answers. We had either to give Japan peace on the Potsdam Surrender Terms or deny peace to Japan while the allies quarrel about what shall be done with what Japan is prepared, and required, to give up. Clearly, the wise course was to proceed now, so far as Japan is concerned, leaving the future to resolve doubts by invoking international solvents other than this treaty."[11]

The delegate of the United Kingdom remarked:

> "The treaty also provides for Japan to renounce its sovereignty over Formosa and the Pescadores Islands. The treaty itself does not determine the future of these islands."[12]

The USSR refused to sign the Treaty. It objected, among other things, to the provision regarding Formosa and the Pescadores:

> "...this draft grossly violates the indisputable rights of China to the return of integral parts of Chinese

territory: Taiwan, the Pescadores, the Paracel and
other islands.... The draft contains only a reference to the renunciation by Japan of its rights to
these territories but intentionally omits any mention of the further fate of these territories."[13]

It is clear from these and other statements made at San Francisco, that although the Treaty provision constituted an appropriate act of renunciation by Japan, the future status of Formosa
and the Pescadores was not considered to have finally been
determined by the Peace Treaty.

The Senate Committee on Foreign Relations also took this
view. In its Report on the Treaty dated February 14, 1952, the
Committee stated:

> "It is important to remember that article 2 is a
> renunciatory article and makes no provision for
> the power or powers which are to succeed Japan
> in the possession of and sovereignty over the
> ceded territory.
>
> "During the negotiation of the Treaty some of
> the Allied Powers expressed the view that article 2 of
> the treaty should not only relieve Japan of its sover-
> eignty over the territories in question but should
> indicate specifically what disposition was to be made
> of each of them. The committee believes, however,
> that this would have complicated and prolonged the
> conclusion of the peace. Under the circumstances it
> seems far better to have the treaty enter into force
> now, leaving to the future the final disposition of
> such areas as South Sakhalin and the Kuriles."[14]

Although China was not a party to the San Francisco Treaty,
a separate Treaty of Peace between the Republic of China and
Japan was signed in Taipei on April 28, 1952.[15] Article II of that
treaty provided:

"It is recognized that under Article 2 of the
Treaty of Peace with Japan signed at the city of
San Francisco in the United States of America on
September 8, 1951..., Japan has renounced all
right, title and claim to Taiwan (Formosa) and
Penghu (the Pescadores)...."

Explaining this provision to the Legislative Yuan, Foreign Minister Yeh of the Republic of China stated that under the San Francisco Peace Treaty "no provision was made for the return [of
these islands] to China." He continued:

"Inasmuch as these territories were originally
owned by us and as they are now under our control and, furthermore, Japan has renounced in
the Sino–Japanese peace treaty these territories
under the San Francisco Treaty of Peace, they are,
therefore, in fact restored to us."[16]

At another point, Foreign Minister Yeh stated that "no provision
has been made either in the San Francisco Treaty of Peace as to
the future of Taiwan and Penghu."[17] During the interpellations
of the Sino–Japanese Peace Treaty in the Legislative Yuan, the
Foreign Minister was asked, "What is the status of Formosa and
the Pescadores?" He replied:

"Formosa and the Pescadores were formerly Chinese territories. As Japan has renounced her claim
to Formosa and the Pescadores, only China has the
right to take them over. In fact, we are controlling
them now, and undoubtedly they constitute a part of
our territories. However, the delicate international
situation makes it that they do not belong to us.
Under present circumstances, Japan has no right to
transfer Formosa and the Pescadores to us; nor can
we accept such a transfer from Japan even if she so

wishes...In the Sino–Japanese peace treaty, we have
made provisions to signify that residents including
juristic persons of Formosa and the Pescadores bear
Chinese nationality, and this provision may serve to
mend any future gaps when Formosa and the
Pescadores are restored to us."[18]

Chinese Mutual Defense Treaty

Against the background of a Chinese Communist propaganda campaign in July, 1954 for the "liberation" of Taiwan, supple-
mented in September, 1954 by military action against Quemoy
and other offshore islands, the United States and the Republic
of China signed a Mutual Defense Treaty on December 2,
1954.[19] The first paragraph of Article V of the Treaty reads:

> "Each Party recognizes that an armed attack in
> the West Pacific Area directed against the territo-
> ries of either of the Parties would be dangerous to
> its own peace and safety and declares that it would
> act to meet the common danger in accordance
> with its constitutional processes."

Article VI provides that for the purpose of Article V the term
"territories" shall mean in respect to the Republic of China, "Taiwan and the Pescadores." In an exchange of notes accompanying the Treaty, there appears the statement, "The Republic of
China effectively controls both the territory described in Article
VI of the Treaty...and other territory."

In its report on the Treaty, the Senate Committee on Foreign
Relations discussed the question of the true status of Formosa
and the Pescadores:

> "By the peace treaty of September 8, 1951,
> signed with the United States and other powers,
> Japan renounced 'all right, title and claim to For-
> mosa and the Pescadores.' The treaty did not specify

the nation to which such right, title and claim passed. Although the Republic of China was not a signatory to the Treaty, it recognized that it did not dispose finally of Formosa and the Pescadores....

"...he (Secretary Dulles) informed the committee that the reference in article V to 'the territories of either of the Parties' was language carefully chosen to avoid denoting anything one way or the other as to their sovereignty.

"It is the view of the committee that the coming in to force of the present treaty will not modify or affect the existing legal status of Formosa and the Pescadores. The treaty appears to be wholly consistent with all actions taken by the United States in this matter since the end of World War II, and does not introduce any basically new element in our relations with the territories in question. Both by act and by implication we have accepted the Nationalist Government as the lawful authority on Formosa.

"To avoid any possibility of misunderstanding on this aspect of the treaty, the committee decided it would be useful to include in this report the following statement:

> ["]It is the understanding of the Senate that nothing in the treaty shall be construed as affecting or modifying the legal status or sovereignty of the territories to which it applies."[20]

In presenting the Committee's report to the Senate on February 9, 1955, Senator Walter George referred to the question of the legal status of Taiwan:

> "The view was advance during committee's consideration of the treaty that it may have the

effect of recognizing that the government of
Chiang Kai-shek has sovereignty over Formosa
and the Pescadores. On the one hand, reference
was made to the Cairo Declaration which stated
that Japan was to be stripped of her island territories in the Pacific and that territories stolen
from the Chinese such as Formosa and the
Pescadores shall be restored to the Republic of
China. On the other hand, reference was made
to the fact that while Japan renounced all right,
title and claim to Formosa and the Pescadores,
such title was not conveyed to any nation. After
full exploration of this matter with Secretary
Dulles, the committee decided that this treaty
was not a competent instrument to resolve
doubts about sovereignty over Formosa. It
agreed to include in its report the following
statement[:]

It is the understanding of the Senate
that nothing in the present treaty shall be
construed as affecting or modifying the
legal status or the sovereignty of the territories referred to in article VI. (SIC)

["]In other words, so far as the United States
in concerned, it is our understanding that the
legal status of the territories referred to in article
VI, namely, Formosa and the Pescadores—whatever their status may be—is not altered in any way
by the conclusion of this treaty."[21]

Quemoy and Matsu

It may be well to note the special status of the offshore
islands, the Quemoy and Matsu groups, in contrast to that of
Formosa and the Pescadores as described here. The offshore

islands have always been considered as part of "China." As Secretary Dulles explained in 1954:

> "The legal position is different…, by virtue of the fact that technical sovereignty over Formosa and the Pescadores has never been settled. That is because the Japanese Peace Treaty merely involves a renunciation by Japan of its right and title to these islands. But the future title is not determined by the Japanese Peace Treaty nor is it determined by the Peace Treaty which was concluded between the Republic of China and Japan. Therefore the juridical status of these islands, Formosa and the Pescadores, is different from the juridical status of the offshore islands which have always been Chinese territory." (underscore added)[22]

Recent Restatement of United States Position

The position of the United States was set forth by the State Department in connection with the 1970 Hearings before the Subcommittee on United States Security Agreements and Commitments Abroad of the Senate Committee on Foreign Relations (91st Cong., 2d Sess.):

> "Legal Status of Taiwan as Defined in Japanese Peace Treaty and Sino–Japanese Peace Treaty
>
> "Article 2 of the Japanese Peace treaty, signed on September 8, 1951 at San Francisco, provides that 'Japan renounces all right, title and claim to Formosa and the Pescadores.' The same language was used in Article 2 of the Treaty of Peace between China and Japan signed on April 28, 1952. In neither treaty did Japan cede this area to any particular entity. As Taiwan and the

> Pescadores are not covered by any existing inter-
> national disposition, sovereignty over the area is
> an unsettled question subject to future interna-
> tional resolution. Both the Republic of China and
> the Chinese Communists disagree with this con-
> clusion and consider that Taiwan and the
> Pescadores are part of the sovereign state of
> China. The United States recognized the Govern-
> ment of the Republic of China as legitimately
> occupying and exercising jurisdiction over Taiwan
> and the Pescadores."[23]

The future relationship of Taiwan to mainland China and the resolution of disputes dividing the governments in Taipei and Peking involve issues that the United States cannot resolve. We have made clear that our primary concern is that these issues should be resolved by peaceful means, without resort to the use of force. Until such a resolution is achieved we may continue to deal respectively with the Government of the Peoples Republic of China and the Government of the Republic of China on mat-ters affecting mutual interests, accepting the practical situation as we find it.

July 12, 1971

[1] Treaty of Peace Between Japan and China, May 8, 1895, 1 Recueil des Traites et Conventions entre le Japon et lese Puissances Etrangeres 375.

[2] A Decade of American Foreign Policy, 1941–1949, at p. 22.

[3] Id., at p.49.

[4] Id., at p. 625.

[5] II American Foreign Policy, 1950–1955, at p. 2448.

[6] XXIII Dept. State Bull. 5 (1950).

[7] U.N. Doc. No. S/1716.

[8] U.N. Doc. No. A/1373.

[9] U.N. Doc. No. A/1381.

[10] U.S. TIAS 2490; 3 UST 3169, 3172; 136 UNTS 45, 48, 50.

[11] Record of the Proceedings of the Conference for the Conclusion and Signature of the Treaty of Peace with Japan, at p. 78, Dept. State Publication 4392 (1951).

[12] Id., at p. 93.

[13] Id., at p. 112.

[14] S. Exec. Report No. 2, 82d Cong., 2d Sess., at p. 8. American Foreign Policy 1950–1955, at p. 470.

[15] 138 UNTS 3.

[16] Despatch No. 31 from the American Embassy in Taipei to the Department of State, July 23, 1952, Enclosure 2, at p. 1.

[17] Id., at p. 2.

[18] Id., Enclosure 3 at p. 4.

[19] U.S. TIAS 3178; 6 UST 433; 248 UNTS 213.

[20] S. Exec. Report No. 2, 84th Cong., 1st Sess., at p. 6, I American Foreign Policy 1950–1955, at pp. 962–3.

[21] 101 Cong. Rec. 1381 (1955).

[22] XXXI Dept. State Bull. 896 (1954).

[23] Hearings, Part 4 (Republic of China), at p. 948 (1970).

Contributors

The Honorable Robert E. Andrews (D–NJ) is a member of the House Select Committee on Homeland Security; its Subcommittee on Cybersecurity, Science, and Research and Development; and its Subcommittee on Intelligence and Counterterrorism. He is also a member of the House Committee on Education and the Workforce, a member of its Subcommittee on 21st Century Competitiveness, and ranking minority member of its Subcommittee on Employer–Employee Relations.

The Honorable Steve Chabot (R–OH) is member of the House Committee on the Judiciary; a member of its Subcommittee on Commercial and Administrative Law and Subcommittee on Crime, Terrorism, and Homeland Security; and chairman of its Subcommittee on the Constitution. He is also a member of the House Committee on International Relations and its Subcommittee on Asia and the Pacific and Subcommittee on the Middle East and Central Asia.

Thomas Donnelly is Resident Fellow in Defense and National Security Studies at the American Enterprise Institute in Washington, D.C., and author of AEI's *National Security Outlook*. He has also served as Executive Editor of *The National Interest*, Editor of *Army Times*, and Deputy Editor of *Defense News*. His most recent book is *Operation Iraqi Freedom: A Strategic Assessment* (AEI Press, July 2004).

William Kristol is editor of the *Weekly Standard* and chairman of the Project for the New American Century. He co-edited, with Robert Kagan, *Present Dangers: Crisis and Opportunity in American Foreign and Defense Policy* (Encounter Books, 2000). He also served as chief of staff for Secretary of Education William J. Bennett during the Reagan Administration and as chief of staff for Vice President Dan Quayle during the first Bush Administration.

John J. Tkacik, Jr., is Research Fellow in China Policy in the Asian Studies Center at The Heritage Foundation. His 23 years of experience with the U.S. Department of State included service in Guangzhou, China, as Deputy U.S. Consul General and in Washington, D.C., as the department's Chief of China Analysis.

Arthur Waldron, Ph.D., is Lauder Professor of International Relations in the Department of History at the University of Pennsylvania. He is also an Associate in Research at the Olin Institute for Strategic Studies at Harvard University and has served as Professor of Strategy and Policy at the U.S. Naval War College. Among his many books is *The Great Wall of China: From History to Myth* (Cambridge University Press, reprinted 1992).

Acknowledgments

This book would not have been possible without the whole-hearted support of the Asian Studies Center at The Heritage Foundation, especially of Harvey Feldman who gave me the inspiration for the volume, and Peter Brookes who urged me to make it a top priority. Larry Wortzel and Ann Klucsarits found the financial resources for the project, and to them goes particular appreciation. Thanks also to my scholarly colleagues, Arthur Waldron, Ross Terrill, Tom Donnelly, and Bill Kristol, for intellectual and moral support in tackling the controversial "One China" dogma.

Special thanks to Heritage interns Will Dorsey, now at Oxford University, and Augustine Lo, now at Cambridge University, for their research support. It is a measure of our special relationship with the United Kingdom that some of our best interns move on to study in England.

But my most heartfelt thanks go to the editors who have made my prose readable and corrected typos and inconsistencies throughout. Richard Odermatt, The Heritage Foundation's Senior Editor, gave thoughtful advice on the text's structure. Senior Copy Editor William Poole saved me from infelicities of expression and caught inconsistencies in Romanized renderings of Chinese names. Jonathan Larsen kindly made this project a priority in the busy Publishing Services schedule, and Senior Desktop Publishing Specialist Alex Adrianson provided the book's attractive layout and cover design.

Finally, sincere thanks to the many contributors and supporters of The Heritage Foundation, whose generous support makes our work possible.